THE POWER OF A GODLY GRANDPARENT

Leaving

a

Spiritual

Legacy

STEPHEN & JANET BLY

BEACON HILL PRESS
OF KANSAS CITY

Copyright 2003
by Stephen A. and Janet Chester Bly

ISBN 978-0-8341-2037-2

Printed in the
United States of America

Cover Design: Michael Walsh

Library of Congress Cataloging-in-Publication Data

Bly, Stephen A., 1944-
  The power of a godly grandparent : leaving a spiritual legacy / Stephen and Janet Bly.
    p. cm.
  ISBN 0-8341-2037-2
  1. Grandparents—Religious life. 2. Grandparenting—Religious aspects—Christianity.
I. Bly, Janet. II. Title.

BV4528.5 .B57 2003
248.8'45—dc21

2002014687

10 9 8 7 6 5 4 3

To Carl and Carolyn Crouse,
our grandchildren's other grandparents,
with much gratitude for their partnership
in passing on a spiritual legacy

Contents

Acknowledgments

We extend many thanks to all our special friends—grandparents, parents, and grandchildren—who contributed their experiences to the making of this book.

1

The Power of
Seeking God First

Within five minutes of meeting Harold and Marti, we heard about their grandson Eric. And no wonder. His accomplishments are inspiring. At 19, he was the youngest in his class to graduate from a prestigious Connecticut university, and his grade-point average earned him the honor of summa cum laude. He earned his master's degree in Scotland, his doctorate from Switzerland. He spent two years helping engineer and construct sanitary water systems in the jungles north of Puerto Bahia Negra, Paraguay.

That's where he met Nicole. Her family lives in Chartres, France. They own a perfume company, among other holdings. Eric and Nicole have two-year-old twin daughters, Elita and Ninete. He is now a full professor in the same university from which he graduated. They spend their summers in Paris. Harold and Marti just got back from a delightful trip there. They even had slides to show us of their family and the trip.

We've known Curt and LaVonne for more than 20 years. They have been long-distance friends for most of that time, the type you get four-page letters from twice a year to catch up on all the family news.

Well, not quite all.

Three years ago we first heard about their grandson Patrick. One of Curt and LaVonne's daughters, Patrick's mother, had been married and divorced before we met them. We had never known for sure about that previous family. It turns out that Patrick was the only child from that marriage. He had gone to live with his father at age seven. Curt and

LaVonne tried to maintain contact Patrick over the years, even though their former son-in-law was antagonistic and sometimes hostile to them. They sent Patrick cards, presents, letters, and put him at the top of their prayer list.

Influenced by his father and his environment, Patrick developed a very expensive drug addiction. While high on drugs, he robbed a mini-mart and shot and crippled the clerk. He is serving 25 years at a prison near Corcoran, California. His is not the type of story that grandparents share slides about.

The good news for both sets of grandparents is that neither story is over yet. Eric still needs Harold and Marti, and Patrick still needs Curt and LaVonne.

Yet this is not the most important thing.

As much as we love our grandchildren, as much as they still need us, there is something more important for every grandparent.

Jesus said, "Seek ye first the kingdom of God, and his righteousness; and all these things shall be added unto you" (Matt. 6:33, KJV).

Grandchildren are added things—not the first thing.

When we were new parents, it dawned on us that we had no idea how to be good parents. In our early 20s with two children, we were anxious about how we could succeed with a family in this turbulent world. So we tried something we had never done before: we read the Bible together.

Neither of us had much spiritual knowledge nor had we attended church with any regularity. We had no Christian friends.

We dug through a box of our old high school annuals stored in the garage and found a promotion Bible that had been given to Janet at a Nazarene Sunday School she visited as a child. We started in and read every night all summer long. By the end of summer, we knew we needed more instruction. That led us to attend a church and sign up for a Bible study. It was a Navigators-based study called "Introduction to Christ."

Within weeks, we individually accepted the truth about Jesus and invited Him into our lives. That was more than 35 years ago. Matt. 6:33 was one of the first verses we memorized as new believers and one of the guiding principles of our new-found spiritual life.

It still is.

There is *one* first thing.

Seek ye first the kingdom of God. The kingdom of God is the rule and reign of Jesus Christ in the lives and hearts of believers right now. There can never be anything else first in our lives —ever.

And all these things will be added unto you. All else are added things.

And God has added wonderful things to our lives. He's added material things we never expected to have. We live at 4,000-feet elevation in the ponderosa pine trees of north central Idaho next to a lake in the middle of the Nez Perce Indian Reservation. We're an hour from the nearest McDonald's and two-and-a-half hours from the nearest interstate highway. We have a trilevel house, a garage, a shop, and a bunkhouse.

Next to the house is a false-front western town (like a movie set) that Steve built. It's a fun place for picnics, cookouts, campfires, and concerts. North of that homemade town is our barn, corrals, and horses.

But these are all added things—not the "first thing." They aren't even close.

Seek ye first the kingdom of God, and his righteousness; and all these things shall be added unto you.

The Lord has also added vocations to our lives. It is our privilege to both be full-time writers. Between us, we have written approximately 100 books and hundreds of articles, stories, and scripts. In addition, Janet is a music director, choir leader, and a professional writing instructor. Stephen has the added responsibilities of pastoring the only church in our little town of 300, and after years on the city council, he now serves as mayor.

But all these are added things.

Seek ye first the kingdom of God, and his righteousness; and all these things shall be added unto you.

We have received thousands of letters and E-mails from wonderful people who have enjoyed our writing. We've been featured on radio interviews and television shows.

But all those are added things.

Seek ye first the kingdom of God, and his righteousness; and all these things shall be added unto you.

In the Lord's grace He has added wonderful friends. In 30 years of pastoral ministry, we've had the privilege of pastoring three churches peopled by sincere, loving, faithful men and women of God. They've worked alongside us, nurtured us, loved us, and looked after our family.

We have dear Christian friends in almost every state, the kind of people you can call in the middle of the night with heartbreaking concerns and know they will physically and spiritually stand with you. It's difficult to imagine our lives without friends like these.

Yet they're all added things.

Seek ye first the kingdom of God, and his righteousness; and all these things shall be added unto you.

One of the delights of our Christian walk is to see how the Lord has added spiritual ministry and blessings to our lives.

Janet travels around the country speaking at women's retreats. Steve speaks at conferences, camps, colleges, and churches. In every location, the Lord is at work and graciously allows us to be a part of what He is doing.

But ministry, as important as it is, is not the first thing.

Seek ye first the kingdom of God, and his righteousness; and all these things shall be added unto you.

The Lord has been especially gracious in adding to us a wonderful family. Ours is a story of high school sweethearts who never stopped "going steady." We have three handsome, smart, witty, loving sons—Russ, Mike, and Aaron—each committed to the Lord. Our youngest son just graduated with honors in political science from Northwest Nazarene University. We have two beautiful, loving, talented, Christ-centered daughters-in-law—Lois and Michelle. We have two sets of in-laws who love the Lord and are delightful to be around (the Crouses and the Thomases). And we have two awesome grandchildren—Zachary and Miranda—who keep our refrigerator covered with photographs and artwork.

And yet with all the overwhelming love these family members bring, with all the many delights they provide, they're not the first thing.

Family is an added thing.

Seek ye first the kingdom of God, and his righteousness; and all these things shall be added unto you.

The Lord is in the process of adding things to our lives. That's what He promised to do.

What He has added to your life might be different than what He has added to ours, but no follower is given an empty barrel. He fills each of our lives with the things that bring meaning and purpose.

That's what He means when He says, "I have come that they might have life, and that they might have it more abundantly" (John 10:10, KJV).

But they're all added things.

Grandchildren are added things. Good grandparenting requires that we keep first things first.

Seek ye first the kingdom of God, and his righteousness; and all these things shall be added unto you.

Remember Eric the college prof? And Patrick, serving time in prison? There's a little more to their stories that you should know.

Harold and Marti pray for Eric, Nicole, and the twins every day. There are several things that trouble them. One thing is that their grandson and Nicole have never married. Marti and Harold worry about what that means for their great-grandchildren.

An even greater worry is Eric's total rejection of God and his antagonism to the Christian faith in which he was raised. Harold's blood pressure goes up every time he ponders some of the things that Eric has said. And Marti's heart breaks when she hears of her darling little twins being instructed in a New Age pantheism.

On the other hand, Curt and LaVonne have been praising the Lord. Last September their Patrick discovered a western novel on his bunk when he came back from the exercise yard at prison. It was written by a Christian and was a story about a man just out of jail in the Old West who was trying to find meaning and purpose to his life. He found that meaning and purpose in a relationship with Christ.

Patrick decided he needed to do the same thing. He has been in triweekly Bible studies ever since he committed his life to Christ, and the prison chaplain recently asked him to teach a Bible study. Curt and LaVonne have visited him many times and describe the tears that flowed down his cheeks when he said "Grandma and Grandpa, forgive me for messing up my life and bringing you so much grief. I'm serious about Jesus. This isn't a jailhouse game."

OK—which sets of folks are the good grandparents? The answer: both of them.

They have both worked hard all their lives to show love, concern, and support to their children and grandchildren. They have demonstrated their faith and have been open with their prayers. They have sought the rule and reign of Jesus in their lives and in their family.

They have sought first the kingdom of God.

With the help of the Holy Spirit, the guidance of the Bible, and the grace of the Lord Jesus, they have provided a legacy, a spiritual heritage, for their grandchildren. Their grandchildren need only accept it.

None of us grandparents can do anything more. And none of us should do anything less.

2

The Power of Your Role as a Grandparent

*Grandchildren are God's compensation
to us for growing old.*
—Anonymous

The last terrific grandmas died just before the war. Well, that's not true—but grandparenting has changed some.

In those "olden days," grandparents were general practitioners. Grandpa could shoe a horse, crank a Model T, build a barn, plumb the house, catch the biggest lunker in the lake, and discuss world politics—all in the same week. Grandma could fashion a formal for her daughter, put up four dozen quarts of peaches, help the milk cow deliver a calf, tack up a starburst quilt, whip up a batch of fudge, and sing all the words of the "Hit Parade's" top 10 songs—all in the same day.

Nowadays we tend to specialize. Granddad is a vice-president or CEO. Or he's the line supervisor. Or he owns a minimart. Grandma sells real estate or manages a dress shop or takes cases to court.

But those examples reflect changes in our society, not in grandparenting. Even in the highly computerized, mobilized, impersonalized gathering we call modern society, good grandparents exist.

The problem is that our world is different than our grandkids' world. Steve grew up, for instance, with one set of grandparents across the street and the other two doors down. Today's grandparents rarely live within an hour of their grandkids. However, grandkids still need grandparents, and it's important to be the best grandparents possible.

We surveyed dozens of grandkids with the question "How are grandmas different from mothers?" and "How are grandfathers different from fathers?" The following answers tell the story.

Grandmas—
Give me things
Hug a lot
Keep feeding me
Accept me just like I am
Want me to explain things they don't understand
Like to smooch
Say things like "A few cookies before dinner won't hurt anyone"
Believe I can grow up to be anything I want to be

Grandpas—
Tell great stories
Laugh a lot
Get sicker than dads
Don't get embarrassed when you do something silly
Need more naps
Let you do things others say you aren't old enough to do
Can tell you what you ought to do without it sounding like a lecture
Know how to say "I love you" with their eyes
Think that you are the greatest kid in the world

Grandparents provide a role model in a child's life no one else can.

Grandparents Can Give Their Grandkids . . .

Family Culture
Sure—Mom and Dad can take time to explain the family ethnic, geographic, or regional heritage, but it can sometimes sound like a parents-versus-kids conflict.

Junior says, "Come on, Mom. Nobody in my class goes to the cemetery on Memorial Day. Everybody goes to the beach." Mom replies, "We're going with Grandma and Grandpa. Grandma's only brother was killed in World War II, and your Uncle Bob, whom you never knew, was shot down in Vietnam. It's our way of saying thanks. We haven't forgotten."

"But, Mom . . ."

"Sorry—that's the kind of family we are."

Parents and grandparents instill a pattern for life. To project a clear direction for the future generation, we need more than one reference point from the past. Parents can provide one; grandparents provide the other.

Family Security

This great big world sometimes seems bent on making life miserable for a kid. In what appears to be a hostile world, a child's home should provide a safe haven. Grandma and Grandpa's house doubles the security. With both sets of grandparents, the feeling of sanctuary is tripled.

A friend of ours reported, "One time I got lost in a big department store. I was sure that my mom had gone home without me. Since she would still be on the freeway going home, I called my grandmother from a pay phone. She talked to me for a long time. Then my mother walked by looking for me. I was so happy to see my mom that I just hung up on Grandma. I'm not sure what I expected her to do, since I lived in San Diego and she was in Houston."

A child thrives with more than one source of stability and security.

A Sense of History

To raise and support a family often demands so much from parents that there's no time to slow down and look at the past. Grandparents add depth, meaning, and flow of the family story and purpose to a child's world.

Sure, Dad once saw Michael Jordan's three-pointer at the buzzer, but Granddad remembers when there weren't any three-pointers at all.

Mom remembers Princess Di's wedding, but Grandmother saw the newsreel when Queen Elizabeth was crowned.

Dad might remember life before compact discs. But Grandpa can tell you about life before color television.

Grandparents bridge the abyss between the facts of history books and the news of today.

A Second Opinion

Good friends are hard to find. Someone to talk to who's on your side and who cares about the whole story is a treasure. In a strong family, parents take time to listen. But on occasion a youngster longs for another view. A little doubt creeps into his or her mind about whether Mom or Dad really understands. Grandma and Grandpa can lend another ear.

Missy stops by her grandparents' for a chat. "Mom says I ought to wait two more years before I get my ears pierced. What do you think, Grandma?"

Grandma smiles. "Well, honey—that cute hairstyle hides your ears anyway."

Grandpa adds, "Missy, you've got to take it easy on the boys. You're so adorable now that they're all heartsick."

"You really think so, Grandpa?" She searches his eyes for sincerity.

"Honey, you remind me of your grandmother the first time I saw her. She was about your age, and I was up on a ladder stocking a shelf when she and her father walked into the store. I thought I was going to fall off the ladder. So you take it easy on the fellas."

The ideal grandparents support the parents' decisions but also affirm the grandchild.

A Bigger Audience

Most everyone likes playing to a packed house. It's great to do your best in front of lots of witnesses. It's also scary. Whether it's the preschool Valentine program, the piano recital, or the graduation speech—there's the possibility of messing up as well as nailing it. So Marcia searches the crowd. She's looking for someone to stand and cheer when she does well or for a good supply of arms to wrap around her if she chokes.

Look out there, Marcia. Do you see Mom and Dad? Oh, wow! Look again—there's Grandma and Grandpa! The adrenaline pumps. She's ready to take on the world. OK. Here goes.

Life's Extras

Some parents can afford to buy their kids everything, but other parents can't or won't. So along come Grandma and Grandpa. They've stabilized their income and own everything they need. They've saved up a little extra for emergencies.

They're primed for presents. You know, those critical things in life like designer jeans or an interest-free loan or the green folding bills tucked into a letter. What else have they slaved for all their lives?

Someone to Help View Parents as Human

When a child begins to think that Mom or Dad were cut from an alien mold, their perception of themselves may become confused: *Do I really belong in this family?*

"I could never be like my mom," Missy moans. "She's always so cool. She never gets excited. She doesn't blurt out dumb things like I do."

Then she goes to Grandma's.

Grandma says to Missy, "Did I ever tell you about the first time your mother decided to cook breakfast? She caught the bacon grease on fire. So she grabbed the frying pan, still flaming, and ran down the street to the fire station yelling at the top of her voice, 'Fire! Fire!' After the firemen put it out, she realized she was wearing only her shorty pajamas. She called us from the fire station to bring her bathrobe and drive her home. She never walked past that fire station again."

Missy replies, "My mother did that?"

Grandparents reveal the rest of the story.

Bragging Rights

Kids like to be proud of their parents. From, "Well, my

dad's a policeman" to "My mom's president of the PTA," kids garner peer points from their parents' roles and careers.

Grandparents can add to the arsenal of healthy pride. "My grandma brought me this from Florida" makes one feel like a seasoned traveler while attending second grade in Chicago.

"My grandpa shook the president's hand."

"You ought to see the meringue on my grandma's lemon pie. It's two feet at least!"

A grandparent's accomplishments, skills, and experiences filter down to add depth to a grandchild's bag of brags.

Kids need grandparents, but they need active grandparents—grandparents who are not satisfied with watching them grow up from some far, distant bleacher.

Active Grandparents	Passive Grandparents
call their grandkids	wait for the grandkids to call
know the grandkids' sizes	
ask to baby-sit	send a gift for the whole family
mark grandkids' special events on their calendars	
	baby-sit only when asked
have the next trip to visit the distant grandkids planned	read about special events in a letter after the fact
display the latest school picture in their wallets somewhere	see the grandkids only when they stop by the house
can name their grandchild's very best friend	toss the latest school picture into a box
	don't try to keep up with their grandkids' ages and grades

Good grandparenting doesn't just happen. Just because someone calls you Grandma or Grandpa doesn't guarantee that you fill the role. It takes some effort. We've discovered five qualities common with grandparents who are serious about improving the art of grandparenting.

Good Grandparents Demonstrate a Spiritual Dimension

Grandparents who have a daily, personal relationship with the Lord God of the universe possess a distinct advantage. They call on Him for help. They glean wisdom from His Word. They're open to the conviction of His Spirit. They're privy to the resources of His power.

In addition, they comprehend the eternal perspective of life and are conscious of their influence on the generations to come.

Nonbelievers can be good grandparents, too, but there's an entire realm of experience missing. Without the spiritual dimension, life can't be known in all its range of truth, in all its fullness.

For years we picked up copies of *Arizona Highways* and enjoyed the beautiful photographs of the Grand Canyon. Especially attractive to us were the shots of the colorful expanse of canyons with a sprinkling of fresh snow. Yet even those professional-quality photos revealed only two dimensions of the canyon. We didn't know what we were missing.

Then, one January we drove to Arizona, turned north at Williams, and headed to the south rim of the canyon. We arrived in the adjoining village late at night and checked into a motel. We set the alarm early so we could spend a full day at the canyon. The next morning we were greeted by six inches of fresh snow.

We entered the canyon right behind the snowplow, ahead of the tourist busses. We parked the car and hurried out on the point to personally experience the Grand Canyon winter. We gasped in awe. We seemed to shrink as we got lost in the splendor of the magnificent sight before us. The magazine photos lacked the depth and enormity of the canyon.

That's similar to the difference between spiritual and nonspiritual worldviews. The dimension of eternity and God's plan for individuals and families and nations is missing. Grandparents who grasp a spiritual perspective open heaven's window for their grandchildren to glimpse more of what life is meant to be.

Good Grandparents Continue
to Grow in Their Faith

Remember the chores you did as a kid that the present generation doesn't have to do? You washed dishes and cars by hand, pushed the lawnmower, rode a bicycle to get around town. Kids today consider those as hardships.

Grandparents whose faith consists of nothing more than a decision made years ago tend to relegate their spiritual journey to a past era too. "Sure, religion was important when Grandpa was a boy," grandkids can say, "but it just doesn't fit us now."

A grandparent whose faith is an active, growing, daily experience demonstrates a viable freshness that works now, that invades the present age.

A growing faith flexes to grasp new insights about the Lord and His part in our changing world. Growing faith doesn't guarantee that you'll have all the answers. But an active faith will help you find them. Faith that's still growing produces a lifestyle of relying on God's daily guidance.

We can test whether our faith is stagnant or not. When the grandkids come over and the subject turns to religion, do we give only examples of experiences from decades ago or from some distant relative? Or do we include what God is doing today, right now?

Good Grandparents Still Have Adventures

There's great comfort in routine.

That's what we work hard to achieve. We endured hectic deadlines and stressful schedules. Been there, dug that rut. We burned the noon-hour oil and took on extra jobs to make bill day less stressful. We set aside many of our own needs for the sake of the kids. Now it's our turn, so don't rock the hammock. We have one obsession on our minds: peace—the relaxed life, space, time of our own.

We want to enjoy the grandkids—without the pressures.

"Don't bring the grandkids over between five and six. That's when Grandpa walks the dog."

"We'd love to see them Thursday, but that's Grandma's club night."

"I know the grandkids would love to go to Disneyland, but I've already stood in enough lines to last a lifetime."

There's nothing wrong with setting boundaries. In fact, it's healthy. But good grandparents muster the strength and courage to plunge into new activities. There's no retirement from grandparenting.

"Mom, guess what?" Natalie blurts out. "Grandpa took me to a rodeo!"

Mom looks over the top of her glasses. "A what?"

"A rodeo. You know, with horses and bucking bulls and clowns and men roping steers and girls racing around barrels."

"Your grandpa never went to a rodeo in his life," replies the skeptical mom.

"Yeah, I know. But I wanted to go, and he said he had 'a hankerin' to mosey on down there' himself. Mom, what do *hankerin'* and *mosey* mean?"

It means Natalie has one adventurous grandpa!

Good Grandparents Understand Their Own Importance

Unless circumstances dictate otherwise, Grandma is not a backup mom, and Grandpa is not a substitute father. An entirely separate category is reserved in our hearts for our very own grandma and grandpa.

Good parents nurture their offspring with the stuff of survival—food, clothing, shelter, education, as well as love—every form of sustenance within their capability. It's in the parenting manual: kids need care.

But grandparents are crucial too. Good grandparents think through this question: "What do my grandchildren and their parents need most from me that I am capable and willing to provide?"

Good grandparents assess the parents' time commitments.

They ask about the grandkids' activity schedule and then analyze their own involvement and figure out where they fit in their grandchildren's world. On occasion, vacation schedules are rearranged or purchases are postponed. Sacrifice is no stranger to a grandparent.

Active grandparents find a void they can fill and fill it.

Good Grandparents Are Willing to Be Misunderstood

When Ethan visits "Grams" and they end up at a department store sale to buy him a new winter jacket, his mother asks Grams, "Didn't you think we could afford to keep our kids in warm clothes?"

The grandparents take their daughter's kids on vacation, and their son complains, "Why didn't you take our kids too?"

Grandma offers to watch the children on Thursday nights, and her daughter-in-law snaps, "We already have a capable baby-sitter—thank you."

There's no doubt about it: grandparenting isn't always smooth. As in all relationships, tempers flare, the timing's off, we don't do things the way other grandparents do. We blow it. We say something we shouldn't have said, and that statement will be carved over the doorway of our grandchildren's home for posterity. Attempting to be a good grandparent requires risk and courage. But the alternative is to walk away and ignore the kids.

Scriptural Foundations for Good Grandparents

How does a spiritual person become the best grandparent possible? By opening a Bible to see what God has to say on the subject. But the scripturally astute among us will protest, "There's no specific passage that describes the perfect grandparent. There's no equivalent to the Prov. 31 verses for women, or Paul's Ephesians 5 verses for husbands and wives."

That's true. However, a close companion can be found in Titus 2:2-5, where Paul declares behavioral standards for the mature citizen within God's family. Follow these to model the effective grandparent.

Basic Attitudes for Grandfathers

"Older men are to be temperate, dignified, sensible, sound in faith, in love, in perseverance" (Titus 2:2).

Temperate: Sober in judgment, self-controlled in temperament, steady in responses—the opposite of overindulgent. Balance in all things is key. The temperate man is one who has learned to reign in passions and enjoy genuine, lasting pleasures, not ruled by appetites or enticed by the slick, the gaudy, the alluring.

Dignified: Serious in faith, respectful of all persons, gracious under fire but not stodgy or out of touch. The dignified man lives with the knowledge that heaven watches. His behavior inspires admiration because he's not like those who have no reverence.

Sensible: Prudent in choices, rational in opinions, wise in decisions. The prudent man feels with a mind that's intact. Younger men struggle with their thought lives, are overwhelmed with temptations and unbridled instincts. The mature man develops inner disciplines. He has tasted God's forgiveness and discovered His deliverance. As Paul wrote in 2 Cor. 10:5, "We are taking every thought captive to the obedience of Christ." What was once a distant goal is now a closer reality.

Sound in Faith: Trusting in God, holding orthodox beliefs, having an honest, personal, daily interaction with the Almighty. Such a man has known griefs and sorrows, as well as triumphs and joys, and has found God faithful. No longer tossed and thrown by debilitating doubts, he is sound in faith and relies on God's Word for stability and courage. Situations that once were seen as debilitating are now embraced as necessary disciplines. Heaven's promise is like an old friend, bringing comfort and companionship.

Sound in Love: Being a powerful dispenser of God's love. One of the greatest dangers of growing old is to slip into bitterness, cynicism, and faultfinding. The opposite should be true. When we recognize our own faults, our own mistakes, and our own failures, we develop within us sympathy and tolerance for others. Having experienced how little true, unselfish love is shown in this world, we should desire to share such love with others. The mature man models God's patience and tender care toward imperfect humans.

Sound in Perseverance: Exhibiting fortitude, the strength that comes through long years spent in active Christian service. Through all the struggles, trials, tears, and victories, God reigns. Let the arrows fly, let the accusations come, let the war games begin. The mature man stands, having done the necessary spiritual calisthenics. His body may waste away, but his spirit stays sharp. The finish line is too close for him to give up now.

Basic Attitudes for Good Grandmothers

"Older women likewise are to be reverent in their behavior, not malicious gossips nor enslaved to much wine, teaching what is good, so that they may encourage the young women" (Titus 2:3-4).

Reverent in Behavior: Practicing love, respect, and awe of God. A mature spiritual woman tames her tongue at the grocery store and in prayer meeting. She knows she walks with God. Jesus is her best friend. She's immersed not in religion but in a relationship with Christ.

Not Malicious Gossips: Content with who she is and her place in God's family, with humble, Christlike love for all her neighbors. Gossip is a game based on pride. It's the desire for superiority run amuck. A woman filled with God's kind of love can't stomach it.

Not Enslaved to Much Wine: Refusing to be controlled by dependency on harmful substances. Older women, especially those without husbands, fight loneliness and long for purpose. Depression grinds away at those who don't feel needed anymore. Boredom zaps the joy of life. Alcohol relieves the agony for some. We can broaden this guideline to include chemical dependencies and any other activity that produces a glazed mind, an addictive stupor.

Teaching What Is Good: Sharing the wonderful truths of the Christian life. Paul views every older woman of the church as a potential teacher—not necessarily a classroom teacher, but one who takes advantage of every opportunity to share truth. The subject matter? All that is good. "Finally, brethren, whatever is true, whatever is honorable, whatever is right, whatever is pure, whatever is lovely, whatever is of good repute, if there is any excellence and if anything worthy of praise, dwell on these things" (Phil. 4:8). And the students? Mainly young women (Titus 2:4). Any pupil He brings to us. Often these will be our own grandchildren.

Titus reminds us that the family of God needs the counsel, the service, the teaching, the example of the older generation of believers. Certainly our own family is included.

But who can be a faultless grandparent? None of us does it right all the time, no matter how long we've followed the teachings of Christ. We're still in the process of being perfected, becoming like Him. However, one young friend of ours thinks his grandparents come pretty close:

Grandma and Grandpa have a great big yard where I can do anything I want. I can jump in the leaves, build a fort, or make roads in the dirt.

I don't think Grandma plays many games with Grandpa, because every time I go over to their house, Grandpa stops what he's doing and wants to play with me.

Then Grandma goes into the kitchen and starts to cook us something. Not in the microwave either. She invents things herself, like double-fudge oatmeal chewies.

Grandma has a great big fat book, and the pages are sort of worn out, but it has wonderful stories in it, and she always reads me one or two (sometimes more). Then I get to sleep in a big bed and have the room all to myself.

I think my grandparents are the best in the whole wide world.

P.S. But Grandma does make me brush my teeth, and Grandpa made me eat some okra, once. Yuck!

Letters like this prove that the grace of a grandchild's love covers a multitude of warts. Grandparents who major in amassing a spiritual legacy leave the richest inheritance of all.

Three Projects for Good Grandparents

1. Go to the phone as soon as you can and call the grandchild whom you haven't seen or talked to for the longest time. Find out what he or she has been doing. No matter how old this grandchild is, end the conversation with "I love you."

2. In the next several days, write to each of your grandchildren. Include in your letter a description of how you used to spend your days when you were their age. Write enough that they get a feel for life back then.

3. Purchase another pocket-sized address book. Compile the names, addresses, phone numbers, clothes sizes, hobbies, and favorite foods of each of your grandchildren. If you have photos, glue them in. This is your "grandkids' book," to be taken with you every time you go to the store, on a trip, or to a meeting.

3

The Power of Making Your Grandchildren Feel Special

Grandparents are meant to stoop—to a child's level.
—Eric Wiggin

The pink dress in the showroom window had a hefty price tag. Melanie's mother explained that such a dress was not practical for a five-year-old who's growing out of her sizes every six months and that the dresses on sale at the department store for half that price were just as nice.

Daddy was tired of eating at the Burger Barn. The hamburgers are too greasy, the milkshakes too thin, and the fries taste like soybean paste. Sure, they have a playground, but he can't stand the thought of eating there again so soon. "Melanie, we're not going," he firmly told her.

When Melanie asked if they could go to the movie together, both Mommy and Daddy groaned: "It's too dark." "The floor's too sticky." "It's always so crowded in there." "The popcorn's so salty and too expensive." "It's too hard to find something decent." "We'll wait and rent the video."

Then Grandma and Grandpa stopped by. They volunteered to entertain Melanie while Mom went shopping. When Mommy got home, she found this note: "We went for a ride—be home soon."

It was 7:15 P.M. when the tired trio barged through the back door. Melanie was ecstatic.

"Mommy, we really had fun. We went to the movies. We ate dinner at the Burger Barn. And guess what else?" She yanked out the pink dress.

Then Melanie's mother turned to Grandma with the classic line "Mother! How could you?"

How could she spoil her granddaughter? It's no puzzle. It's fantastic fun.

But *should* grandparents spoil? To spoil implies giving someone better than he or she deserves. Every kid needs a bit of that. The Bible is crammed with accounts of how God spoils us, that is, gives us better than we deserve. It's called grace.

Our sin deserves death—so what does God give us? "The wages of sin is death, but the free gift of God is eternal life in Christ Jesus our Lord" (Rom. 6:23).

A little spoiling now and then might help the grandkids understand God's generosity to us all.

Why Do Most Grandparents Want to Spoil Their Grandkids?

At certain seasons of life, the demands pile up. Life is harried, and there's no time to ruminate—only to react. A mom with preschoolers, for instance, rarely relaxes in the recliner to ponder family history.

One benefit of getting older and having your own children raised is to consider the past and what it has to do with today.

On a foggy morning just south of Santa Cruz, California, Steve was vacationing with his maternal grandparents. Grandma Wilson woke him up to say, "Little brother, it's time for breakfast."

Steve knew that meant eggs, bacon, homemade biscuits, and gravy. Steve remembers Grandpa Wilson sitting at the table reading the newspaper while waiting conspicuously in the corner of the room were two fishing poles, a bucket, a fish knife, and a box crammed with hooks, yarn, and little fake bug-like creatures of bright colors and wild designs.

Nothing had to be said. Steve knew what was happening after breakfast. He and Grandpa would drive down to where the waves crashed onto the sandy beach. They would climb the stairs to the top of the pier and walk creaky wooden planks out over the thunderous explosion of surf. Then, way out on the end, practically close to China, Grandpa would say, "Sure looks like a good place to stop, don't ya think?" They would spread out the gear and drop their lines. For the next several hours, they'd reel in several dozen "tom cods" and chat about the olden days.

Your memories of your grandfather might be different, but you'll have a similar reaction. You'll walk into the kitchen and say to your wife, "Next time we visit the kids, I'm taking Sam to the pier."

"I don't think he has any fishing equipment," she says.

"Well, I'm going to buy him some. A seven-year-old boy ought to have his own fishing gear. Know what I mean?"

She knows. She knows you're about to spoil your grandson.

Now, some might insist, "I never knew my own grandparents. How can thoughts about them influence me now?"

But that very fact should motivate you to see that the same thing does not happen to the next generation. Start your own traditions. Take a grandchild into the wilds of your choice.

Spoiling grandkids has a lot to do with economics. Contrary to what most kids think, not all grandparents are rich. But most grandparents like to spend whatever they have on the grandkids. That makes for an agreeable arrangement.

How we spend our money changes over the years. Our son Michael and his wife, Michelle, have a passion to buy a new car and a speedboat. They spend weekends at car and boat dealers trying to find a great bargain on upscale models. But Michael's older brother, Russell, and his wife, Lois, scan the newspaper every week searching for a bigger family-friendly house to purchase that will include space for her daycare center and a room to home school their kids.

As for us, we have our permanent home. We're not interested in more toys. Our pickup and Chevy run just fine, and we'll never need another bedroom set or coffee table or set of silverware. The sizes of our clothes don't change much, and we have no compulsion to follow the fads. If we look a tad dated, that's fine with us. We don't have anyone to impress except each other.

All the possessions we thought we had to have during the first 25 years or so of marriage we have either managed to purchase or live without. Besides, the closets are jammed, and the garage is crammed. We don't need more stuff.

It's a curious phenomenon that for a lot of us our pay scale peaks about the time the kids are all grown. There's more time, more money, and fewer personal needs. What a setup! Here we are, ripe plums ready to be plucked by some of the cutest, brightest, most terrific kids in the world—our grandchildren.

"Sure, I could buy myself another golf bag," a friend told us, "but I'm used to this old red jobber that's followed me around the course all these years. I'd rather buy Brad that fancy skateboard he's been moaning about."

Spoiling grandkids sometimes revolves around their current environment. Suppose your 32-year-old son decides on a career change that requires two more years of school. He plunges into the books, and his wife grabs the best job she can find. They manage to pay the bills somehow, but that's about it. Meanwhile, Melinda, Marcy, and Mark have to cut back on some of the extras.

Along come Grandma and Grandpa. "Grandpa says he'll send us to camp." "Grandma's going to help me get my cheerleading outfit." "Grandma and Grandpa think we need a riding lawnmower for this huge yard."

Sometimes the grandchildren may need our time and attention to get through serious difficulties. Maybe there is obvious neglect. Maybe they're caught up in a custody battle. Perhaps your son is laid up for six weeks after surgery, or your daughter is struggling through a difficult pregnancy. Perhaps one of your grandchildren's parents dies.

Good grandparents know when to enter center stage—and when to exit.

When Anne started teaching art at the college every Tuesday and Thursday afternoon, her mother called. "Honey, can I swing by and pick up the children after school and have them stay with me?"

"Well, sure, Mom—if you insist," Anne replied.

"Would it be an inconvenience if they had dinner with Dad and me on those nights?" her mother added.

"Oh, well, you know—if you insist," Anne responded as she plotted a quiet dinner for just her husband and her.

On May 21 the semester ended. It was also the last of the two afternoons-a-week stints for Grandma, at least until next September. She gracefully bowed out.

Once you're free from the day-to-day responsibility of raising your own children, it's prime time for spoiling the grandchildren.

When Grandma attended Abby's fifth-grade play, she was "simply delighted" with her granddaughter's performance and how darling she looked in her tree costume. She gushed on and on about "our little actress."

But Abby's mom had been nagging Abby for weeks to sit still and practice those lines. And when Mom looked at the costume, she thought of the three nights of sewing until midnight only to be told that the 100 tiny green leaves would have to be replaced with brown ones. She also grimaced at the pizza sauce stain on the trunk that got there because Abby insisted she put the costume on before supper. And she saw a daughter who pouted for a month because Jessica was selected for the leading role "even though everyone knows I'm better."

Ah, the joys of not being Mother!

On Tuesday afternoons and Saturday mornings, Dustin's dad plays catch with him. While that's a very good record, Dustin would like to play catch every night. He doesn't understand the compelling call of yard work, balancing books, committee meetings, and just plain exhaustion.

"Grandpa Powers plays ball with me every day when he comes to see me," Dustin insists. "How come you can't?"

Of course, Grandpa only makes it by a couple times a month. You see, that's the ecstasy of grandparenting. We might not be there all the time, but when we are, we can make the kids the center of attention.

Sometimes it's difficult to exercise our spoiling rights. As an example, the situation is more complex if we still have some of our own kids at home. It's difficult to spoil one or two kids when there are others still living under full-time house rules. We call this "hamstrung grandparenting," and it calls for modifications in the role as "spoiler."

Complications intensify when your grandchildren live with you. When an unwed teenage mother raises her baby at home along with her siblings, the guidelines of grandparenting must change. Or if your married son and his spouse and children move in with you while their new house is being built or to survive a layoff, that presents a special set of circumstances that must be approached differently. Stephen deals with these types of situations in detail in his book *Once a Parent, Always a Parent.*

But those of us who can spoil without creating havoc in our homes do so simply because we can—because we're closer to the finish line.

Grandparents come in all ages. Janet's mom was only 34 when Russell, her first grandchild, was born. We were 46 when Zachary arrived. But whatever the age, becoming a grandparent enlightens our perspective on what's important in life.

Dave and Patsy were devastated when Kayly received a "D" on her report card. They discussed grounding her, enrolling her in another school, hiring a tutor, and appealing her grade to the school board. For more than a month, every time she got home from school they barraged her with questions about how she did in biology that day.

Grandma has heard all about it from Kayly's parents. But when Kayly stopped by, not a word about grades was mentioned. She received hugs and kisses and the usual plate of warm oatmeal cookies. Then Grandma let Kayly prattle on about girlfriends, boys, and pesky sisters.

Grandma cares about Kayly's grades. But she realizes that

one bad grade does not a delinquent make. She can't remember what grades her own children got in biology. But she does know that one failure doesn't predict total failure.

Grandparents can spoil because they understand what they missed out on.

"Dad, nobody in this part of the country wears a hat like that. Why did you buy Quinton a $50 cowboy hat?"

"Son, I'm 64 years old. I've wanted to own and wear a hat like that since I was five. I reckon Quinton doesn't need to wait that long. Looks pretty good on him, don't you think?"

Treating Grandchildren as Individuals

The Bible advises, "Train up a child in the way he should go, Even when he is old he will not depart from it" (Prov. 22:6).

Grandparents can help grandchildren become the unique persons God created them to be. If our spoiling diverts them from this aim, then we become a hindrance. However, if our spoiling neither prevents nor actually assists them in their God-directed path, then we do no harm.

Note the implication in this verse. "Train up a child in the way *he* should go." Each child journeys a different path in his or her spiritual pilgrimage. That could be a different path than the one followed by his or her parents or grandparents or siblings.

Good grandparents treat each grandchild as a unique individual. Two major obstacles stand in the way of doing that.

First, it's tempting to treat all grandkids the same. One-size-fits-all grandparenting is simpler. Choosing one activity for the whole gang requires less planning, and picking a gift and multiplying it times the number of grandkids takes less time. For some grandparents there are reasons other than laziness for choosing this option.

But here's one way we slip into that mold. While traveling in Colorado in November, Marty and Gertrude Akin stopped at a gift shop. On display were the most adorable red sweatshirts with plush, fuzzy teddy bears on the fronts. "Aha—the perfect Christmas gift for the grandkids." So, they bought five of them.

After Christmas, the Akins realized their mistake. Each of the grandchildren wrote charming, scrawled thank-you notes, but two of the shirts were never worn. The oldest child thinks he's too old for teddy bears, and one of the girls hates to wear red. Sure, they hit the mark on three out of five, "But if we'd given each one a bit more consideration, we could have delighted them all," Gertrude tells us.

Second, treating each grandchild as an individual is not always appreciated, and it can cause complications. If Jared receives a bicycle when he's six, Jamie expects the same. This may or may not be a good tradition to get started. Jamie's maturity, interests, and personal circumstances may override this choice regardless of her age. But chances are that she wouldn't understand this.

And maybe parents won't understand it either. "Mother, I don't know why you sent Billy a box of candy and didn't send one to Linda too."

Well, maybe Linda had told you that she was on a diet, and you hadn't really planned on sending anything to either child. But then you heard about Billy's not making the baseball team and knew how crushed he would be, so on an impulse you sent him his favorites: chocolate-covered cherry bombs, which Linda doesn't like anyway. You thought you had all the bases covered.

Responding to an individual grandchild's need is a tricky thing. On the other hand, we have one not-to-be-underestimated resource going for us: things like this can be overlooked and soon forgotten because "that's just the way Grandma and Grandpa are."

Here are some hints for spoiling your grandkids in all the right ways.

Spoiling Grandkids Good

Change a Few Habits

Try to think of ways to single out each grandchild as an individual. Address a letter by specific names. Instead of writing, "Dear Rob, Ginny, and kids," try "Dear Rob, Ginny, Ryan, Richard, Rachel, and Rebecca." It takes a few seconds longer, but they might notice. Kids love to see their names in print and in letters.

By doing this, we grab their attention. They don't see it as just Mommy and Daddy's letter. It's their letter, too, and there's news for them. They feel Grandma really wants to know about what's going on with them too.

Even better, include a personal note to each grandchild. "You've got mail" is a thrill to kids too. They still believe that no bad news comes in a mailbox. They don't receive bills, pink slips, or jury summons yet. A card, a gift, or an occasional letter or E-mail brings instant delight.

Start Another Recipe File

On the alphabetized tabs with your index cards, list your grandchildren by name: Then record recipes and food items each one enjoys. Amy devours your taco casserole. Bridgette refuses cold carrots but tolerates them cooked. Chad must have ketchup on his hot dogs.

Of course, if you have only one grandchild and a great memory, you might not need the file. But most of us need all the help we can get. Cheat sheets like this can make Grandma and Grandpa seem like sheer geniuses.

The real secret is to review the list before the grandkids come over. Plan menus around some of their favorite dishes. While grandparents are allowed to introduce new foods once in a while, it's not our job to get little Chad to try broccoli. If he demonstrates disgust for the horrid green stalks, we can feed him corn instead.

One grandma we know goes to extremes in this area with satisfying results. Whenever the grandkids come over, Ruth prepares a separate meal for each of them. One gets a hamburger and tater tots, another gets a shrimp salad, the third is served pepperoni pizza, and the last receives a peanut butter, raspberry jam, and banana sandwich on wheat bread.

We asked Ruth if it was a big hassle cooking different

things for each of the kids. "Because they live so far away, my grandkids come only once or twice a year," she stated. "Here I am, usually alone in this big house, eating my little microwave dinners. This gives me a chance to cook again—and I figure going out of my way to please my grandkids won't hurt them or me one bit."

It pleases her daughter too. "All my kids talk about on the long drive to Mother's is, 'What will Grammy Ruth cook for us this time?'"

Plan Your Calendar a Year in Advance

Time spent with grandchildren depends upon several key elements—the number of miles between you, the total number of grandchildren, their ages, your health, and their parents' attitudes.

Even in the most restricted cases, the possibilities for time with the grandkids increases when we plan in advance. So, pull out the calendar and start marking.

Here's the goal—to spend personal impact time with each grandchild, alone, at some point in the next year. "Personal impact time" means getting to know each one better without competition and without interruption.

A week with each grandchild each year is ideal. Janet remembers that one of the most pleasant memories of her childhood in a large, poor, single-parent home was to have a week of her grandparents' undivided attention. It's not always possible to single each one out for one-on-one time, so here are sample goals to aim for:

If you have—

1 to 5 grandchildren, at least one weekend per year;

6 to 12 grandchildren, at least one day per year;

13 to 25 grandchildren, at least half a day per year;

26 or more grandchildren, at least one evening per year.

Some grandparents have contact with their grandchildren every day, but they're the exception. If this is a privilege you enjoy, your grandchildren may get all the individual attention they want and then some. In this case, it may be necessary to use their time with you to have them tag along for running errands and checking in on friends and keeping assorted appointments. Otherwise, these distractions are best kept to a minimum.

That's why we need the calendar. When we coordinate our commitments, special days, and events with theirs, here's what it might look like.

In June, Herbert and Helen Hunter attend an American Legion convention in San Francisco. Their son and his family live in San Jose, so they make plans to spend some time with them. Their son has two daughters: Hanna, 13, and Heidi, 9. Herbert and Helen want individual impact time with Hanna and Heidi, so they plot out their convention schedule, double-check with the girls and their mother, then plan a strategy.

On Friday, the Hunters pick up Hanna, drive back to San Francisco, and do some shopping along Fisherman's Wharf. That evening they have dinner together at a fancy restaurant.

On Saturday, it's Heidi's turn. Grandma and Grandpa Hunter pick her up for a morning at the zoo. For lunch, it's hotdogs in the park. That afternoon they go to the aquarium. That evening, the whole family's invited to eat out.

But what about Hugh? He's the grandchild who lives in a condo on the north shore of Lake Michigan. Herbert and Helen make arrangements to swing by his place on their way to Cheyenne Frontier Days during the last week in July. They'll introduce him to horses, cowboys, Western art, parades, and carnivals. This kind of summer may be wearing, but why are they saving their energy if not for the grandkids?

The activities need not be complicated or expensive. Chances are, your grandchild will love a whole morning at the playground. "Watch me jump, Grandma. This is really high, don't you think? Catch me, Grandpa."

When your grandparent calendar is completed, some of the events may have to be switched around. Flexibility prevents many grandparenting hassles. But once the dates have been duly detailed, your year is on target for being there for your grandkids.

When Janet's mother died, the family realized that some grandparent duties are gender sensitive. Grandpa Chuck handed Janet her mother's grandparent calendar with all the special dates for their large, extended, blended family marked. "Send this info out to all the kids and grandkids for me, please. Your Mom did all the card and gift buying," he said. "I can't keep up with it, so I won't be doing anything for Christmas or birthdays."

But he had an alternative idea. "I'm getting the motor home overhauled and I'll take a trek across the country from Montana/Idaho to Vegas, from California to Florida, to see each one of you. All I have to give anymore is myself."

Give Gifts for No Reason at All

Let's dispense with the obvious. Birthdays require compulsory gifts, and they must be on time. We know that, and the grandkids expect it. Kids think they deserve a Christmas and birthday present. It's in the grandparenting contract somewhere.

So why not add a clause to that contract? How about a present for no reason at all?

First, count the grandkids and set yourself a budget. Determine what would be a reasonable amount for each gift.

Suppose you could afford $10 a month for this extra, and you have 12 grandchildren. Each month one of the grandkids discovers a card that says, "I was thinking of you," and a trinket or toy from Grandma and Grandpa. There's none of the holiday or birthday pressure. Just keep an eye out for "Grandma and Grandpa" goodies. You might find one at the supermarket, another at the golf course. It doesn't take long to train the brain to be on the alert for such items.

Four-year-old Melodie marched into the preschool classroom carrying a $3 orange giraffe. During show-and-tell time she showed off her newest possession.

"His name is Gerald," she said. "Grandpa sent him to me."

"Is it your birthday?" a little friend asks.

"Nope."

"Well," he asked, "why did you get a present?"

Melodie shrugs her shoulders. "Well, Grandpa says Gerald gave him the saddest face. He needed a little girl to play with, and Grandpa thought of me."

But what about grown grandchildren?

Treat them the same. But send them car wax or bags of miniature Hersey bars or colored tennis balls or tins of assorted flavored popcorn or a phone card. Adult grandkids enjoy surprises too. Small serendipities like that say, "I love you."

We can give gifts to our grandchildren spiritually as well.

In Gen. 48:9—49:28, elderly Jacob blesses his grandsons. Why can't grandparents today, in our society, bless their grandchildren?

In a certain sense, only God can truly bless. If blessing means to impart a spiritual benefit, then we all fall short. But blessing can also mean to acknowledge certain qualities, talents, and gifts in another (*Theological Wordbook of the Old Testament* [Chicago: Moody Press, 1980], 1:132., s.v. "*bār-ak*"). A grandparent can thank and praise God publicly for positive qualities in their grandchildren.

Look for opportunities to publicly make such benedictions.

A granddaughter's 12th birthday or a grandson's 13th is a transition time. It's a good time to impart a positive blessing statement. If it's impossible for you to be there at the celebration, write down your feelings and have someone read them out loud. And if you have reason to believe you might not live to celebrate these milestone birthdays, then do it as soon as you can.

Special words of praise coming from the heart of a loving grandparent could provide a piece of the rock of character the child needs to cling to during the turbulent teen years.

Grandkids need to be blessed, so spoil them spiritually.

We received a note from our grandchildren's other grandparents in which they blessed us and our grandchild:

We are so pleased that Miranda has you to explore the wonders of God's creation with her. That little girl is either going to be a botanist or a horticulturist or a writer like her Grandma and Grandpa Bly. We hope the latter. She is so eager about exploring things and creating ideas. When they were here with us in California, both Zachary and Miranda loved to explore the bugs and the leaves and all the new growth in our backyard. It was so neat to see their enthusiasm over what we had long classified as trivial.

We can never tell a family member too much how they have benefited our lives.

Gifts for Peace Offerings

"Then Esau ran to meet him and embraced him, and fell on his neck and kissed him, and they wept" (Gen. 33:4). This is one of the most poignant scenes in the Bible. Jacob deceived his brother and stole his birthright. Then he fled from home when he heard Esau threaten to kill him. Many years and hard lessons later, Jacob determined to return home. But first he had to confront his brother. Jacob experienced fear and trepidation as they met again. He brought a peace offering to soften his brother's heart and to try to amend his treachery. "Please take my gift which has been brought to you, because God has dealt graciously with me and because I have plenty," he told Esau (Gen. 33:11).

Luisa faced a similar type of situation with her son, Brian. Upset by a comment she made about his parenting of his three children (her grandchildren), Brian wrote her a long letter listing a series of grievances he felt hadn't been addressed, beginning with Luisa's divorce from his father. Luisa was devastated. She thought she and Brian had a loving relationship. But burning issues had simmered beneath the surface for years. After some months of cooling and a number of letters back and forth, Luisa was to meet with Brian and the children at a restaurant halfway between their two homes in hopes of a face-to-face reconciliation. She searched for just the right gifts for this "nonholiday" situation. "I didn't want it to be too lavish yet not trivial. The kids knew little or nothing about the war of words and feelings between their grandmother and father, but I felt something needed to be restored between us. For Brian and for each of the children I wanted a token offering that would affirm my love and be symbolic of my desire for forgiveness and peace between us."

Gifts like this are the most challenging of all. Luisa sought the wisdom of God and did find some presents that seemed right, but she also determined that her changed attitude was the most important gift.

4

The Power of Loving
Long Distance

*If nothing is going well,
call your grandfather or grandmother.*
—Italian proverb

We hadn't visited with Chet and Rosanna for almost 10 years. It was great to discover them at a conference in Michigan. After preliminary laughs, hugs, and chatter, we got down to the important talk.

"How's the family? What are the kids doing now?"

Chet spoke up first: "Oh, they're all doing great! Matt and family are living in Houston. He's with NASA. They have a big house out at Lake Jackson and three of the cutest girls in Texas."

Then it was Rosanna's turn: "Did you know our Bobby was in the Air Force? Well, he married a darling girl from Sweden. They live up in Connecticut on a beautiful old farm. He flies transport planes and has twin boys."

"How about Sandra? Did she make it through med school?" we asked.

"Oh, yes," Rosanna said, smiling. "She lives in southern California, has a practice in Malibu, and teaches at UCLA. She's married and expecting her second child in February. We still haven't gotten to see her first child, Jason, but they're so busy they never get away.

"Wow!" we replied. "They've all really done well."

Chet shrugged. "Yeah, I'm really proud of them. But Texas, Connecticut, and California are a long way from Grand Rapids. We try to see them all once a year, but it's getting harder and harder."

Rosanna sighed. "When we were younger, we used to make all these plans about what we would do with the grandchildren. But they're just too scattered. It would be great to have them all live a little closer."

I wish our grandkids lived closer. Bring up the subject of grandchildren with any group of grandparents, and you'll likely hear this lament.

With that in mind, we asked dozens of grandchildren, "If you could instantly change one thing about your relationship with your grandparents, what would it be?"

Ninety percent replied, "I'd have Grandma and Grandpa live closer so we could spend more time with them."

Further investigation revealed that the other 10 percent already live near their grandparents.

Grandparents who consider moving near the grandchildren risk finding themselves caught in a cycle of job changes and advancements that make another relocation likely. So Grandma and Grandpa often stay put and watch their family drift farther and farther away.

Carl and Carolyn Crouse of California found a solution by purchasing another place in a mobile home park in Idaho. They spend half the year in California with the hometown grandkids and the other half in Idaho near our grandkids, who happen to be theirs too.

How Can You Grow Closer
to Your Distant Grandkids?

Try an annual survey. A survey is a good way to keep up with all the gang. One couple we know sends theirs with a stamped, self-addressed, return envelope and $5 worth of McDonald's coupons. They report a 100-percent reply.

A sample questionnaire for the 6- to 12-year-olds might go like this:

   1. Who is your very best friend in the whole wide world? Why do you like him or her best?

2. What are your favorite clothes to wear, and what do you like best about them?
3. What is your favorite game to play this year?
4. What is your favorite part of the Bible and why?
5. What's your favorite television show this year? What day is it on? What do you like about it most?
6. Do you ever get afraid? What scares you most? Why?
7. Who's your hero or your favorite person this year? Why did you pick him or her?
8. If you could pick any job you want when you grow up, what would it be? Why do you like that one?
9. Do you get lonely very often? What do you do when you get lonely?
10. What's your favorite color of clothes to wear? What do you have in your closet that color?

The secret to a good survey is to keep it simple and short. Adapt the questions to the particular child, and provide a varied group of questions. Choose topics that are nonthreatening yet have potential to reveal who the inner child is. Use the survey to keep up on their personal preferences and spiritual progress.

You might ask, "What do you like most about Sunday School?" "What verses have you memorized?" "What was the neatest spiritual lesson you learned at camp?" "What are the three most important things you'd like me to pray about?"

Some of you might complain, "But we have 32 grandchildren. We can't possibly do that for all of them."

Why not?

Do you really have something more important to do than to invest your time and effort in the spiritual interests and personal opinions of your grandchildren?

Try consistent letter-writing. Let's be honest. Grandkids, whether they're 5 or 15 or 25, aren't known to be good letter-writers. There's the occasional exception, but often a scrawled two-line thank-you note at Christmas and birthday time is about the most any of us expect.

If we see our grandkids less than once a month, we can write or E-mail them.

Here's one plan:

1. Communicate one-on-one with every grandchild.
2. Assume you'll average 15 minutes on each letter.
3. Set aside the same time every week for letter-writing.

Taking two hours every Sunday afternoon, you can write to 8 different grandkids each week—32 in a month. If you only have 4 grandkids, write to 1 each week.

If writing is really hard work for you and you would rather pull an acre of nettle weeds out by the roots with your bare hands than sit down and think up something to write, consider it like a job. What if, in order for your grandkids to complete their education, you needed to take on a two-hour-a-week part-time job? What if there were just no alternatives? Most of us would push ourselves to do it.

A serious letter-writing campaign can be a part of their education, and it's part of our inheritance to them. And who's to say which is the most important?

What will you write about? Most will find plenty to say. But if you need some help, here are 12 ideas to stir into the letter-writing ink pot.

January—Share what your daily (and weekly) routine looks like. If you're still working, tell them where you work, when you get there, what you do, what your job accomplishes, and when you get home. If you're retired, chances are you're busier than ever. Tell them about the golf on Tuesdays, volunteer work on Thursdays, the bookshelves you're building for the den, the snow shoveling, working at the hospital auxiliary, or whatever.

Tell them what time you go to bed and how early you get up. Walk them through a day or week, giving them a running commentary of your activities. You want them to have more than just a vague notion of a lady or gentleman rocking in a chair beside the fire.

February—How about an opinion on world news events? They have access to all the facts. They can read or watch television and see what's happening in China, Europe, or around the nation. But what does all this mean to you? Then tell them about that Russian or Arab or Indian family who lived on your block and some of the stories they told you about life in their former country.

If it's an election year, tell them who you've decided to vote for and why. Share with them a particular concern you might have about our country, or share an example of praise for the privileges we enjoy.

March—Describe how things look in your part of the country. Tell them about melting snow, green meadows, tall mountains, flat plains, city parks, and high-rises. Share a vignette about what the land around your home looked like before it was settled. Tell them, for instance, how your nearby lake is similar to the ocean they live next to or how it's different. Tell them one thing you like best about this season of the year.

Tell them about the trees, the flowers, the soil, the crops, the gardens, whatever features capture your interest or theirs.

April—Tell them something of your personal struggles and successes. Write at their level but share what you're learning from the Lord. They need to know that the Christian faith is a growing relationship. It's all right for them to find out that Grandma and Grandpa don't know everything yet. Tell them about answered prayers. Share a verse that means a lot to you, and tell them why. Tell them about the most exciting new spiritual truth you've discovered.

Even if your grandchild is being raised in an unspiritual family, he or she will be interested in what's happening to you personally. Share a testimony you heard, or relate a project that your church family is doing. Describe an interesting Christian you have met.

This might be the place to share about famous people who happen to be Christian. If little Billy loves baseball, tell him about the major league pitcher who's a preacher during the off-season. Include a news clipping or two.

May—Recall a memory from your childhood from when you were their age. Tell what your school was like, how much homework you did, who your best friend was. Tell them how you got to school and what happened if you were late. Tell about what games you played at recess and what you wore to school. Confess to them about the kid you envied the most, and tell why.

Plunk your grandchildren down beside you in that classroom and describe the whole scene. Help them feel the hard wooden seat and hear the screech of Jim Summer's fingernails across the chalkboard.

June—Send them a yearly survey that you've filled out yourself. Answer the same questions you asked them. Tell them about your best friend, how the relationship came about, and what it means to you. Tell them about your favorite color for clothes, your most-watched television show, your shoe size.

Ask your grandkids to make up their own survey and send it to you. If they do this, you have a ready-made topic for the next monthly letter.

July—Tell them about a memorable vacation. One grandma relates the first time she saw the Pacific Ocean. She rode for six days on the train to the West Coast, then ran out with her good shoes still on and stood in the breakers. It ruined her shoes, but she never forgot that moment.

Tell them about the people you traveled with, the scenery, the activities, the people you met along the way, and what was happening in your life at the time.

A grandpa tells about the wilderness camping trips he took because his family was too poor for anything else, and the time his rich uncle paid his way to Europe when he graduated from high school.

August—Give them a review of a book you've read that you think they might like, or go to the bookstore and ask the clerk which are the three most popular books currently selling in your grandchild's age-group. Then glance through them and see if they seem appropriate. If they are, buy them. But don't mail them yet.

Read the books yourself. Then tell your grandchild how

you enjoyed the book without giving away the ending. Ask what parts he or she likes most. There are very few statements more authoritative than "My grandma and I think this is a really good book."

September—Get reflective. Share with them why you're looking forward to heaven. Recite your favorite Bible verses about eternity. Give your philosophy about how they can best survive in an evil, imperfect world. Assure them of God's constant, powerful presence and protective care.

"Grandma always liked to talk about spiritual things," your grandchild will say.

Don't hold back your spiritual self. But keep your comments personal and warm, like a conversation with a friend who happens to be your grandchild. Try to keep from sounding like a preacher, even if you are one. Keep it centered on what's real in your own life, not what you expect your grandchild to believe.

An outspoken atheist acquaintance once admitted in private that the one fact of Christianity he couldn't come to terms with was his own grandmother's faith.

"She talked a lot about heaven. On the day she died, that's all she wanted to discuss. In her last hours, she smiled and said she could hardly wait. Every time I've convinced myself that God doesn't exist, Grandma's smile and final words come to my mind. I wish I didn't think of her so often."

Never stop telling them about spiritual truth that's real to you.

October—Ask them their advice. Find a topic they're very interested in, and ask for their opinion.

For instance, suppose you must buy a new car. Poll your grandkids and find out what kind and color they think you ought to get. Be specific about what you're looking for. Tell them you want to find a fuel-efficient four-door that's fun to drive—if that's your style. Or tell them you're leaning toward a 4 x 4 pickup with a stick shift—whatever you want. Even your seven-year-old grandson will have some opinion. "Get a black one," he pleads. Your 12-year-old might try to convince you that you really need a Trans-Am. Your 16-year-old grand-daughter just knows you'll be happy with a red Corvette convertible.

They will all have fun giving Grandpa and Grandma their opinions. When you make the final purchase, tell them why you decided on this one.

Ask them what kind of stereo to buy or which science video they would recommend or which pizza place is the best. Get their opinions on which Saturday night television program is the most entertaining.

Cultivate opportunities for them to offer friendly counsel, and listen to their replies. Kids can be right.

November—Tell them what you're thankful for this year. Jot down a review of how God has supplied your needs and wants. Walk through your calendar month by month, and touch on those special blessings He gave and the tough times He has seen you through.

Tell them how thankful you are that they're a part of your family. Let them know you delight in their friendship. Tell them what you'll be doing on Thanksgiving Day if you'll be apart.

Maybe you have a story about a special Thanksgiving you'll always remember.

December—Get theological. Tell what Christmas means to you. Explain its meaning, that God "became flesh, and dwelt among us" (John 1:14). Make sure every grandchild of yours knows the Christmas story. It's about "Immanuel," "God with us" (Matt. 1:23).

Take the symbols of Christmas and teach one spiritual truth for each. For instance, the angels and shepherds show us the Heavenly Father's watchful care over His children; the star over Bethlehem was God's sign that He wanted our attention and that He was doing something important; the gifts that the wise men brought cause us to consider what gifts we could bring Him; the splash of colorful lights remind us of the great joy of the event.

Janet once taught a weekday class of fifth- and sixth-grade

girls. About once a month they would have a special event, and Janet would send a flyer and note to each girl to describe it.

One week, after the letters went out, a girl named Jody rushed to the class, a wide smile splashed across her freckled face. "Mrs. Bly, your letter was the first mail I ever got in my whole life."

Try meaningful telephone calls. Letters and E-mails are great, but they can't draw you quite as close as hearing a voice. Find the times for the best long-distance phone rates, whether it's evenings, early mornings, or weekends. Figure out what fits with your grandchildren's schedule and when it's the best time for them to talk and not feel interrupted or pulled out of bed.

If finances are a consideration, check your long-distance company. Find out what a three-minute call to each of your grandchildren will cost.

How do you make calls meaningful?

- Think through ahead of time what you're going to ask. Don't call first, then search for something to say. Jot down a note or two so you won't forget.
- Don't ask the obvious. If it's the middle of winter and they live in Alaska, don't ask if it's cold.
- Try not to ask too many questions that can be answered "yes" or "no." Instead of, "Did you have a good day?" try, "What was the most fun thing you did at school today?"
- Tell them you miss them and you love them. They need to hear from your lips, in your voice, that you really care. Don't assume they already know it or have outgrown their need for that.

"Grandma called me last night," Gavin reported.

"Just to talk to you?"

"Yep."

"Well, what did she want?"

"She wanted to know if I thought the Cubs could hold on and win the pennant. I told her if they don't get some help at the plate, they'll fold by Labor Day."

"What did your grandma say?"

"She said she loved me and would call me after the first of September. I've always got to explain baseball to her," Gavin confided with a most serious face. "My grandma needs me to help her."

Smart kid.

Smart grandma.

Try the latest technology. Cassette tapes, camcorders, computers, E-mail, chatrooms, discussion boards, conference calls, cell phones: we have multitudes of devices to communicate with anyone, any time, anywhere in the world. If you don't know how to use something, ask a grandchild!

Suggestions for recording a good tape:

- Decide ahead of time what you want to say.
- Relax. Talk to them as though they're in the living room.
- Reduce as much background noise as possible.
- Ask several questions that will encourage them to send a reply.
- Perhaps use a theme, such as the ones we suggested for letter writing.
- Send a self-addressed, stamped mailer to encourage them to send back their own recorded message.

Film yourself with a video camera. Give them a walking commentary on your yard, your pets. Send them a short clip from your visit to the Blue Devils Air Show. Shoot some footage down the hall where you hung Brad's plaster of paris handprint and Brianna's latest school photos.

Become a serious photographer. About four times a year, grab a role of film, dust off the Instamatic or Polaroid or Nikon, and shoot a roll for the grandkids. Show them Grandma or Grandpa in front of the blooming dogwood tree or singing in the community chorus or whitewater rafting. Remember: it takes a lot of pictures to find a few good ones. You don't have to be the world's best photographer—just get them in focus.

Encourage the grandkids to take pictures as well. Buy them a simple camera if need be, and send them a roll of film and return postage. With double prints, they keep one and send you one with their own comments or detailed explanations.

When the Lord said, "Be fruitful and multiply, and fill the earth, and subdue it" (Gen. 1:28), some families took on the whole burden themselves.

Grandkids can be scattered all over the country and the world. They can be old enough to have their own children or still be in the crib. They might be actors or doctors, politicians or pilots. Some are over six feet tall, and others are less than 100 pounds soaking wet.

But all of them have two things in common: they're related to you, and they need an active grandma and grandpa.

Don't let distance rob them—or you—of this pleasure.

5

The Power of
Your Family History

*If a grandmother puts her foot down, the only safe
place to do it nowadays is in a notebook.*
—Florida Scott-Maxwell

In the spring of 1869 Thomas "Bronc" Barstow helped drive
3,600 head of cattle from the Rio Grande River in Texas to
the railhead in Kansas. After collecting his pay, he rode on to
Omaha, Nebraska, and boarded one of the first interconti-
nental trains west. He left the train at Ogden, Utah, and
worked his way north.

By 1875 Bronc was operating a livery stable in Bozeman,
Montana Territory. It was there he met Katherine Sample,
formerly of Boston, Massachusetts, and the two married. During the 1880s they ran a cattle spread in the Teton Valley of
eastern Idaho Territory. Eleven children were born to them,
but only nine survived infancy. By 1890 the cattle ranch, like
many around them, had gone broke.

The Barstows moved to Spokane, Washington, in the early 1890s and ran a feed store. But when the Nez Percé Reservation opened up for partial white settlement in 1896, Bronc
and Katherine staked out a claim and moved to the Camas
Prairie. The B-B Ranch has been in business ever since.

This is a nice little story, but it won't mean a whole lot to
you. The Barstows are not a famous family. You've probably
never heard of them unless you're an old-timer around Lewis-
ton, Idaho, and remember when Kenny Barstow shot out all
the street lights along Main Street one New Year's Eve.

But this is very important to Lorraine Barstow McDonald. Last winter while sorting through an old trunk of personal belongings left in her grandmother's estate, Lorraine found Katherine Sample Barstow's diary, her grandmother's grandmother.

"I cried when I read it," Lorraine admitted. "The words, phrases, expressions, actions—they were all so classically Barstow. We haven't changed a whole lot in a hundred years. When she wrote about the pain of losing little Susan in the flood of '89, I sobbed. After all, these are my kin. I felt very aware of my place in history, and I felt the desire to carry on a tradition. I went right out and bought a journal so my great-great-grandkids will know the stories I know."

Lorraine is one of the fortunate ones. If we're fortunate, too, perhaps we can remember a few stories that our grandparents used to tell, but that's about it. It's as if the Lord created each family brand-new without any connection to the past.

But He didn't. In fact, God indicates it's important to remember the former days.

"Give heed to yourself and keep your soul diligently, so that you do not forget the things which your eyes have seen and they do not depart from your heart all the days of your life; but make them known to your sons and your grandsons" (Deut. 4:9).

God seems to expect one generation to learn from the previous one. He does not intend to have to reteach every lesson, and He is counting on that heritage to be passed down from family to family.

The Importance of Chronicling Your life

There are two main reasons many persons fail to chronicle their lives for future generations: They think nothing interesting ever happened to them, and they're convinced they have no writing skills.

So you didn't cross the desert in a covered wagon, attend a conference with Eleanor Roosevelt, or step onto the moon with Neal Armstrong. Even if your life story would never be the screenplay for a major motion picture or dime novel, you are the one called to transfer whatever family history you can.

There's a tale about a man named Harvey from central Kentucky around the early 1800s who sought his fortune in New York City. Six years after arriving there, Harvey was prospering as a merchant and trader. He decided to return for a visit to his hometown and friends.

As Harvey got off the stagecoach in Hardin County, Kentucky, he spied a childhood chum. After some preliminary greetings, he quizzed his friend about what had happened in central Kentucky during his absence.

"Oh, Harvey, you know nothing new ever happens here."

"But I've been gone six years. Don't tell me everything's the same."

"Yep. Pretty quiet in this part of the country. This is the backwoods, you know."

"Yeah, I guess you're right—nothing ever happens here," Harvey replied.

"Oh—well, now that I think of it, Mrs. Lincoln had a baby—but that's about it."

"A girl or a boy?"

"A boy. They named him Abraham or something like that."

We don't always recognize significance when it happens. Our historical perspective comes with the passing of decades.

No one alive today can claim our times are dull, boring, or even peaceful. We all need to be keeping journals.

Your granddaughter's granddaughter will roll on the floor laughing when she reads what your kitchen is like, she'll be thrilled at your description of the thick forests and wildflower-covered hills, and she'll shed tears when you describe the way you felt the day your daddy died.

And about your writing skills—you might be right. But what difference does that make? The family history does not have to be submitted to an editorial committee for scrutiny.

Write in your own words in your own way. The reader will

discover your personality from the way you express yourself as well as by what you say. The joy of a personal journal is that there is no bad form.

Here are three suggestions to keep in mind as your begin your journal.

Write legibly. Use the best handwriting you can muster with your skills and health. Type it or use a computer, if possible. If you must write by hand, slow down and make it as legible as you can.

Use top-quality products. Don't use a faint pencil on the back of a shopping bag. Ink fades over the years, and the acids in cheap paper eat away at the text. Invest in a nicely bound blank journal or some top-quality rag content paper so the copy's as clear in 2095 as it is today.

Protect your journal. It's as valuable as anything you own. Keep it in your safe, or store completed volumes in your safety deposit box or fireproof file. Treat it like the treasure it is.

Ideas for a Family Journal

OK—now you're hyped. You zip out to the bookstore and pick up a gold-trimmed, leather-bound, 320-page book of blank pages—now what?

If you're stuck on what to write about, here are a few hints.

Make a Family Tree

In the front of the book, diagram your family tree. It might take several pages and several months to create.

Or start with a big piece of poster board (about 24" x 36"). Then, using a pencil that's easily erased, lay out the whole clan. Start with you and your mate and work down through the kids and grandkids. Print the entire given name of each person, the date and place of birth, and the date and place of death, where appropriate.

On a separate piece of paper compile all family names, addresses, and phone numbers you have. A sample chart appears on the following page.

Husband   **Wife**
born (b)   born (b)
location (l)   location (l)

date married (m)
location(l)

1st child—spouse		2nd child—spouse		3rd child—spouse	
b.	b.	b.	b.	b.	b.
l.	l.	l.	l.	l.	l.
m.		m.		m.	
l.		l.		l.	

children:	*children:*	*children:*
name	name	name
b.	b.	b.
l.	l.	l.

If your grandchildren are married, then add the spouse's full name. And, of course, include any great-grandchildren.

When complete, back up and include your parents, your spouse's parents, and your and your spouse's grandparents.

Where you stop is up to you. If you're related to a historically important person, by all means trace back to them.

Add to the family tree the names of your brothers and sisters, your spouse's brothers and sisters, and their children so that grandchildren can identify their counterparts in other branches of the family tree.

If you possess other data about your family, include it.

When you're finished with the poster board, transfer the information to the smaller sheet in the journal. Record the current list of names and addresses as well. Even though your tribe might be the kind that moves often, this will be a record of where they are at the moment.

Then, if you like, take the smaller copy of the family tree to an instant printer and make enough copies (on bright red or green paper, of course) to send in this year's Christmas card. If you made any mistakes, someone will be sure to point it out. However, few family trees are simple, clear-cut trunks and branches. What about divorce, remarriage, stepchildren, half-sisters, and the like? As a reporter, not a judge, record the facts. The more complicated the family tree, the more helpful the chart.

Another type of family tree for your journal is a spiritual one. It does not need to be as complete as the first. Chronicle a few simple statements about the known spiritual commitment of various family members.

Here's a sample: Grandfather Snively, converted and baptized in Basque County, Texas, 1908. From 1915 to 1927 he served as a lay preacher in Methodist churches. He was Sunday School superintendent at Clinton Memorial Church from 1927 until his death in 1943.

You can't know everything about the faith of each relative, and only God knows for sure what anyone's true commitment is, but jot down what you do know and what has been publicly stated and recorded. Any reader of the Bible senses the importance of genealogies.

In the Book of Ruth the last few verses state that Naomi's grandson, Obed, happened to be the grandfather of King David. Little David did not "come out of nowhere" to slay Goliath and rise to be king. We know much about the character of his great-grandmother Ruth and his great-great-grandmother Naomi.

You might believe you're the first confessing Christian in your clan. However, if you dig back some, you may discover a faithful grandparent or great-aunt. It's a treasure to understand the big picture of what God is doing in our families and to pass that news on to future generations.

We were both 22 years old and the parents of two sons when we came to know Jesus as our Savior. We told our whole extended family of our new commitment. Some were pleased, some noncommittal, and some a bit hostile. But at least one was openly ecstatic—Janet's Grandma Chester.

A year and a half after we committed our lives to Christ, we determined that the Lord wanted us in full-time ministry.

That meant leaving the peace and security of the family ranch, five grueling years of university and seminary work, and then relocation to wherever the Lord wanted us.

Again, some of our relatives rejoiced, some yawned, and some worried about us "going overboard with all this religion stuff."

But Grandma Chester was gratified and delighted. For more than 30 years she had prayed that one of her children or grandchildren would serve in pastoral Christian ministry. We knew nothing of her prayer, but we're thankful that she lived to see it answered. She repeated to us Simeon's words from Luke 2:29—"Lord, now lettest thou thy servant depart in peace, according to thy word" (KJV).

Why did we decide on this particular vocation? It had a lot to do with Grandma Chester's prayers. Make sure future generations of your family know their spiritual heritage.

Write Down Stories of "the Good Old Days"

You don't have to remember everything at once. The beauty of a journal is that you aren't giving a detailed chronological study of your entire life—just a few glimpses of how things were. If you're stumped for ideas, how about including one scene from each decade?

What were the 1940s like? It doesn't need to be a historical account—that can be found in textbooks. But describe in detail one scene from the '40s that you think typifies your experiences. Mary Alice remembers an incident when the baseball team from Lemon Cove rode the train down on a Saturday to challenge the locals to a contest. Buck Hamilton belted the homer to tie the game in the eighth, but the ball bounced onto the highway and into the back of a pick-up truck, as they found out long after. It was the only ball in town, and the game had to be called a tie. Mary Alice says, "We went ahead with our picnic supper and for years afterward argued who was the best team."

Do you have a story from the '50s? Barbara Ann journaled, "We were the first ones in our neighborhood to own a television set. It was quite a marvel—black and white, of course. That was the crazy, early days of live TV. Even commercials were live. It was a riot—like when the saleslady couldn't get the refrigerator door open. Or the newsman thought the sound was turned off. I remember a watch slipped off an elephant's foot and got smashed. I especially loved the variety shows. Sid Caesar and Ed Sullivan were my favorites."

And don't forget your views on the '60s, '70s, '80s, and '90s. Sure, there are plenty around to describe more recent years, but tell your side of the story. We plan to include scenes like the traffic jam on University Drive the day of the campus riots over the Vietnam War and about our last trip to the Grand Canyon and how that experience has changed so much over the past 50 years.

What's happening today will be "the good old days" to future generations. For fun, make a few predictions of your own on how you perceive the future will be. Your grandkids can judge your accuracy. If you're close to being right, they'll shake their heads in awe. If you're way off, they can hoot with glee. Either way, you've reached through the years and touched them.

Write About the Ups and Downs of the Family

In your journal include the sorrows as well as the joys. Seek a balance, and be honest.

"Grandpa and I bought a grocery store on Broadway and 14th," Eunice writes. "Business boomed to the point that the store covered a whole city block. But that wasn't the first store we owned. There was another market down on State Street that didn't do well for us. We lost the house, the car, and our savings when it folded. But God was good, and He gave us another chance."

Describe your thoughts when the Marine sergeant showed up at the front door to tell you about young Bobby's war-front death. Or when the doctor came into the waiting room and announced, "There's just nothing else we can do." Or the day you sold the family home and drove away from it for the last time.

Life is measured by not only the good times but also your responses to failure and sorrow.

Give Answers to Questions They Should Be Asking

The day will come when your offspring will say, "Man, I wish I had asked Granddad or Grandma about . . ." Do them a favor by answering some of those questions ahead of time.

What will they want to know? Think about all the questions you wish you had asked your own grandparents. These ideas might touch off some of your own.

1. Give a room-by-room account of the earliest home you can remember. Describe the layout of the house—the furniture, heating system, kitchen utensils, colors, textures, garage, everything.

2. Describe your grade school, your favorite teacher, and what made this one stand out.

3. When you were a teen, what career did you want to pursue? Why?

4. When and why did you decide that your spouse was the one you ought to marry?

5. What was the smartest—and the dumbest—purchase you made before you were 30?

6. If you had it to do over again, what one skill would you like to learn at an early age? Why?

7. If you could pick out one different era in history in which to live, what would it be? Why?

8. Describe in detail what attending church was like when you were a kid.

9. When you were first married, what did you pay for rent? For a car? For a loaf of bread? For a stamp? What was the pay scale for a good job? How much did you earn?

10. Describe all you know about your own grandparents. What did they look like? What were their personalities? Occupations? Strengths? Weaknesses?

Now we have two more potential projects for you to consider to keep the family history alive.

Describe the Places Where You Have Lived

First, hunt around and find a large map of the United States (or the world, if you need it). Make sure that it's one that's OK to write on.

Mark the different locations where you and your spouse have lived. Put a red X and date by the town. Then, if you have the data, take a different-colored pen and do the same for your parents, your mate's parents, and your grandparents.

At a glance, your family can see the geographical movement of your clan. Maybe the map will help your family see the clan's progression from one place to the other more clearly. Your grandchildren will witness the stability or mobility of your family.

Organize the Family Photographs

Second, go to the closet where all those old photographs are tossed in Buster Brown shoe boxes. Pull them out and identify them on the back. Do it before you've forgotten half the names and can make a close guess on the dates.

- Don't worry about putting them in an album yet, especially if that's the reason you've neglected this project.
- Write on the back of the photos with a soft marker—one that won't fade and that writes easily enough that you don't have to press hard and thus damage the photo.
- List the names of all the people you know, all the objects you can identify (like the car your family drove when you were in first grade), and the best guess you can make of the year you think the photo was taken. Just put a "circa" by the inscription.
- Store your pictures in the safest place you can find.

Recently some friends of ours lost their home to a fire. Forty-six years of possessions were suddenly gone forever, yet the main thing they really grieved over were "the photographs—we can never replace all those pictures."

Try to protect them from floods, fires, earthquakes, tornadoes, and vandals. A fireproof file would be ideal. Don't store them in the garage or kitchen or bathroom. Keep them high and dry. It's more effective to tell your grandkids what life has been like for you when you can show them pictures.

Grandkids who know their historical origins have an advantage. They know who they are. Grandkids who know their spiritual legacy also know why they are and where they're headed.

A journal, a map, a family tree, a file of well-marked photos: these are an inheritance even Bill Gates would envy.

6

The Power of Teaching Your Grandchildren Your Unique Skills

*A grandparent will help you with your buttons,
your zippers, and your shoelaces and not
be in any hurry for you to grow up.*
—Erma Bombeck

It's old, worn, and often covered by a silk bedspread. But on occasion we peek under the covers and look it over again.

It's more than a faded, well-used quilt. The interwoven circles and stitching display the "wedding ring" pattern. But we see something more.

We see a screened-in front porch with four homemade sawhorses and four long, narrow slats clamped at the corners. Stretched between the slats is a large quilt. The frame fills the porch. In one corner sits a gray-haired, bent-framed, soft-spoken former Texas lady, a sweet smile on her face, a silver thimble on her finger. After stooping over that quilt all summer until every stitch was in place, she folded and wrapped it in last year's Christmas paper, ironed smooth. Her payment? A Christmas morning hug.

Grandma Wilson didn't slave like that for money, though she could have used it. Nor did she work for acclaim. Critics might comment on her penchant for using up any old scrap of cloth in the house, no matter what color or texture. There would be no professional color wash.

Grandma made quilts because she wanted her family to stay warm at night. She had this notion that anyone without a warm handmade quilt to wrap up in was deprived. She couldn't provide such comfort for the whole world, but she could take care of this one family.

What used to be custom woodwork on the front of houses has been replaced by molded plastic. The bouquets on dining room tables are now likely made of silk. A laser duplicator from Hong Kong carved the wooden ducks. The corner china cabinet is glued sawdust with a stretched plastic photo of wood grain wrapped over the top and stapled together by a robot.

Where have all the craftsmen gone?

This trend can be reversed in your family, starting with you. Teach your grandchildren some of your own unique talents.

Know Your Talents

"I don't have any of those kinds of skills to pass on," you might say. If that's true, why not learn one?

The truth is, you're probably loaded with talent to share, but you don't recognize it. It's so familiar that it seems ordinary. What we think is routine, because so many in our generation can do it, stands out to those in another age.

Grandma Beulah learned how to hitch a four-horse team and sled through the snow to feed the cows. There isn't more than 1 person in 100,000 in our country today who could hitch up and drive four horses.

Grandpa Clive calls the pie "river bottom custard," because that's what his mother called it. It's made with pecans, tart apples, white raisins, lemon rind, 12 eggs, sugar and molasses, a special mixture of delicate spices, twigs of clove, and takes about five hours to prepare. Grandma Clare got the recipe from Grandpa's mother and offered to teach their married daughter how to make it. "Oh, Mother—you know I just don't have time for things like that," she replied. "Besides, Barry likes the Pie Palace. I'd rather eat out."

So, like the California condor and circus parades, river bottom custard pie will soon be extinct.

For more than 30 years people stopped by Grandma Bea's backyard on Memorial Day weekend and asked, "Do you mind if I cut a few gladiolus to take out to the cemetery?" The answer was always a cheerful, "Help yourself!" Flowers from that famous gladiolus patch of hers used to adorn half the tombstones at Rolling Hills. Grandma Bea's kids never had much patience to learn how to grow flowers. Besides, they had little motivation. They could always come over and enjoy hers. But now Grandma Bea is thinking of moving in a year or two into a mobile home park, one that's mostly green outdoor carpeting and cement. She still has time to teach the grandkids how to grow those gladiolus.

Do you play the dulcimer? Make doll houses? Embroider pillowcases? Paint landscapes? Collect stamps? Shoot a black powder rifle? Write poetry? Breed cocker spaniels? Rebuild old cars? Create Christmas tree ornaments? Lay brick? Knit or crochet? Any skill, with patience, can be transferred to another generation.

If you're having trouble finding your own skills, ask those around you, "What do I do well?" and "What are my special abilities?"

Before you pass from this world, make sure one of your teachable skills is carried on to at least one of your family members.

Know Your Grandkids

From their earliest days, notice your grandchildren's bents, their potentials, their interests. Who exhibits a latent talent similar to yours?

Meanwhile, share tidbits with them from your own abilities.

Our friend Curtis is an accomplished wilderness photographer. He made his living by working for AT&T, but his love was taking pictures. He developed a standard procedure with his seven grandchildren. When each of them turns seven, he gives him or her an inexpensive 35mm camera.

Then he takes that child on an outing to the lake near his

home. He gives him or her lessons on how to take good photos. He supplies the film and pays for developing for any grandchild who wants to further pursue shooting wilderness shots. All he or she has to do is send Grandpa the finished roll of film. He develops it, mails the prints back with a new roll of film, and suggests how each print might be improved.

Out of the seven grandkids, only two have kept it up. Last year 13-year-old Carri sent him a roll every month. He smiles as he talks of Carri: "She's got a photographer's eye, she does." He pulls out a snapshot of a formation of Canadian geese flying a few feet above the water. "I'm getting her a wide-angle lens and a developing set for her next birthday. I wouldn't be surprised if she goes to work for *National Geographic* someday," he brags.

Know Your Business

To teach a particular skill requires some advance planning. Let's suppose you're going to give your nine-year-old grandchild a first lesson in woodworking.

You clean the shop and put up the power tools. Then you select the wood, lay out the pattern, purchase extra safety goggles, check on the carpenter's glue, purchase stain, put a new handle on the hammer, pick up a small pair of rubber gloves, and purchase more sandpaper.

Teaching a skill is more than having the person watch you do it yourself. It's showing the grandchild step-by-step and then allowing him or her to do it. It's challenging your grandchild but not pushing him or her into a process that's too advanced, too overwhelming, too complicated. Set before the person a project that, with a degree of effort, he or she can complete.

Roberto spends so much time in his garage that his car is usually parked out on the street. He builds shelves, picture frames, flower boxes, coffee tables, and hope chests.

In 39 years of marriage he's collected every tool imaginable. He wouldn't think of turning the grandkids loose in his shop, but he doesn't bolt the door to the garage when they come over either. Roberto's plan is like this: If the grandchild is under 5, he or she is allowed to sit on a stool and watch Grandpa work. This lasts about three to five minutes, he reports. The child gets an idea of what he's doing. When the grandchild reaches the 6 to 10 age bracket, he shows him or her how to sand, paint, and pound nails. In his scrap bin full of wood, he finds a simple project. When the grandkids burst through the back door yelling, "Grandpa, do you have anything I can paint?" or "Can I help you pound nails?" Roberto is prepared.

When they are 11 to 15 years old, he teaches them how to use the smaller hand tools such as saws, planes, and chisels. It's also time to learn about some of the power tools like electric sanders, hand-drills, and jigsaws. He encourages them to design their own projects.

At age 16 and above, those who are still interested can handle the big power tools. He leaves the entire project to them from wood selection to the last coat of varnish.

"Do you need any help in the shop, Grandpa?" the kids shout as they meet him at the door.

It's a funny thing: Grandpa always needs help. It's as if he planned it that way.

Know Your Limitations

A 5-year-old grandchild has a limited attention span. So does a 75-year-old grandparent. The projects they work on together must fit them both.

When Alissa was 7, she spent a week with her grandmother at their cabin. Grandma Martha spent the afternoons painting along the river's edge while Alissa played in the sand. Each day Alissa inspected Grandma Martha's work. By the end of the week, the painting was done.

"Grandma," Alissa said, sighing, "I wish I could paint like you."

"I bet you could someday," Grandma encouraged.

"Nah, not me. My teacher, Mrs. Melton, said my art wasn't good enough to hang up for open house."

"She *what?*"

"Yeah, I read stories during art time instead."

That challenged Grandma Martha. Lord willing, and if she lived long enough, she would work with Alissa until she could paint a lakeside landscape.

Of course, a squirmy 7-year-old has a long way to go. So Martha developed an ambitious plan. Each year during their time together, she taught Alissa a different technique. She didn't mention to Alissa where all the lessons were leading. In fact, Martha placed her own lakeside landscape in a closet out of sight.

The first few years were pretty basic, even humorous— little scratches of attempts to draw a tree or a rock. Every year's pictures were placed in a "memory box." The occasional letters to Alissa would contain a hint or two about how to draw better. On her 12th birthday, Grandma Martha sent her a set of oil paints. On her 14th, Alissa got a beautiful wooden easel. On her 16th she received a selection of canvasses and brushes.

In the summer when she was 17, Alissa was once again at the lake. She had quit her summer job one week early to be with her grandmother the week before her college classes began. This time both ladies were down at the lakeside painting.

"Grandma, I've decided to minor in art. What do you think?"

"I think you'll do very well. You could come home and teach me a thing or two."

By Saturday Alissa had almost finished her painting. "You know, Grandma, you probably don't remember this, but I used to hate art."

"Really?"

"Yeah, I didn't think I could do it. I was really embarrassed for anyone to see what I'd drawn. It seems easier now. Did I get that reflection of the sunset on the water bright enough?"

"It's beautiful," Grandma Martha replied.

That evening Martha went to the closet and pulled out a dusty old painting. "Do you remember this?" she asked Alissa.

"No, not really."

"How does the sunset compare with yours?"

"Can I be honest? I like mine better. I think I've captured how the light reflects, then gradually disappears into the waves."

"I agree. I painted this picture 10 years ago. At the time you told me, 'Grandma, that's the most beautiful painting in the whole world. I'll never be able to paint like you.'"

"I said that?"

"Yes. And now you've out-painted me."

"But yours *is* very nice, Grandma."

"Honey, I knew we could prove her wrong."

"Who, Grandma?"

"That teacher who said you couldn't draw."

"Yeah, I guess we did." Alissa hugged her grandmother.

Martha knew her limitations. But she knew she could teach a few basic concepts at a time. She was aware of how little time per year she would be allowed to work with Alissa. And she knew that her granddaughter could accomplish only so much at 8, 9, or 10.

But Martha looked beyond the jam-smeared freckles and the sand-filled, stringy brown hair and was able to see potential that others missed.

Teachers are busy with a whole room crammed with students. Parents are swamped by survival and necessities. But grandmas and grandpas can supply the gift of encouragement and, sometimes, the gift of teaching.

Know What It Will Cost You

Nobody ever said grandchildren were cheap.

Check out their Christmas lists—how many presents do they want that cost less than $10? $20? $50? But being a good grandparent means investing more than money. It may take all your spare time and most of your patience to teach a skill to one of your grandchildren.

Becky will cut the pattern wrong and waste yards of material.

Brett will burn up your new table saw.

Tyler will hoe out all the carrots in your garden and leave only the weeds.

Annie will borrow your 1903 stamp to mail a postcard to Santa Claus.

And Jill will fill your electric drill with glue.

Active grandparenting means losing cookie pans to the chocolate chip crematorium.

It means giving up some golf games.

It means including a tagalong on your trip to Arizona.

It means finding an all-day sucker stuck to the bottom cushion of your sofa.

There's a price for being the kind of grandparent who takes time to teach his or her grandchildren.

Know Your Grandkids' Other Grandparents

Our gifts, talents, and input into our grandkids' lives should never be done with the motivation of competing with the other grandparents or other nurturing relatives, and certainly not to criticize their way of doing things. Ellen had a special problem: she enjoyed sewing and crafts as much as her granddaughter's other grandmother did. Leslie would come to Grandma Ellen's house, and Grandma would say, "Let's make beaded earrings today." Or "I found a great pattern for peasant blouses." And Leslie would often say, "Oh, Nana already showed me that."

Ellen finally found some projects that Nana wasn't interested in that she and Leslie could do together with no threat of overlapping with Nana.

What Scripture Teaches About Gifts

Too many of us have a narrow view of full-time service for God. We limit the choices to pastors, evangelists, church planters, and theologians.

We separate "spiritual gifts" into definite categories and get discouraged if we feel we don't fit any of those.

It's possible, therefore, to read about teaching your grandson to build a decent birdhouse and assume, "My—this isn't very spiritual."

But in Exodus, Moses gathered the Hebrews out of Egypt and marched them into the wilderness. Then God dispensed His laws to them on Mount Sinai. For the first time in their history, they were to have a place of worship. God revealed to Moses the blueprints for the portable worship center. But how would such a masterpiece be built? He would need skilled laborers.

Then Moses said to the sons of Israel, "See, the LORD has called by name Bezalel the son of Uri, the son of Hur, of the tribe of Judah.

"And He has filled him with the Spirit of God, in wisdom, in understanding and in knowledge and in all craftsmanship; to make designs for working in gold and in silver and in bronze, and in the cutting of stones for settings and in the carving of wood, so as to perform in every inventive work.

"He also has put in his heart to teach, both he and Oholiab, the son of Ahisamach, of the tribe of Dan.

"He has filled them with skill to perform every work of an engraver and of a designer and of an embroiderer, in blue and in purple and in scarlet material, and in fine linen, and of a weaver, as performers of every work and makers of designs.

"Now Bezalel and Oholiab, and every skillful person in whom the LORD has put skill and understanding to know how to perform all the work in the construction of the sanctuary, shall perform in accordance with all that the LORD has commanded" (Exod. 35:30—36:1).

Six key points stand out in this passage:

1. *God called Bezalel by name* (35:30).

The Lord didn't say to Moses, "Scout around for your best building contractor." He didn't say, "Moses, don't you have a guy with gray hair and bushy eyebrows who's a pretty good silversmith?"

God knew exactly what skill each one possessed.

Bezalel isn't known in history as a mighty warrior. He didn't slay giants, conquer kingdoms, face fiery furnaces, or utter prophetic words about end times. No Old Testament book is named after him. His name is not included among the heroes of the faith in Heb. 11. But God called him by name.

When the history of the great people of our century is completed, we might not be mentioned. But God still calls each of us by name. As far as He's concerned, Bezalel's work was as important as any that needed to be accomplished.

2. *The Lord filled Bezalel with His Spirit* (v. 31).

We live on the other side of the Cross from Bezalel and on the other side of Pentecost. Quoting the prophet Joel, Peter said on the Day of Pentecost that in our day God would "pour forth of [His] Spirit upon all mankind" (Acts 2:17). We have grown up with the idea that every believer in Christ is allowed access to the Holy Spirit.

But what about the days before Pentecost? It's a rare thing to find mention of any human being "filled with the Spirit of God" before Pentecost. We do find a few—like Moses, Joshua, David, and some others—but we can almost count them on our fingers.

That's why this reference is so startling. Here's a man, Bezalel, filled with the Spirit of God. What does he do with this wonderful power from God? He builds things.

If Bezalel took a modern survey to discover his spiritual gifts, he might be surprised that "craftsmanship" was not on the list.

3. *Bezalel was given wisdom, understanding, and knowledge to do his craft* (v. 31).

This passage elevates all skills and talents. Could it be that there's something God-given in the ability to lay brick? Build fences? Sew drapes? Make goblets? Carve wood?

But then, someone could protest that the spiritual nature of Bezalel's gifts had to do with the project itself—he was called to create a tabernacle for God. So the ordinary, common—even profane—now became spiritual, special, and sacred because of what was being constructed.

According to that theory, if you're using your skill for something dedicated to God, then and only then you are doing a spiritual work. If it's for common, ordinary use, it's non-spiritual.

This argument has a major flaw. Jesus said in Matt. 25:40, "Truly I say to you, to the extent that you did it to one of these brothers of Mine, even the least of them, you did it to Me."

And Paul made it clear: "Whatever you do in word or deed, do all in the name of the Lord Jesus" (Col. 3:17).

Therefore, every use of our God-given skill becomes something dedicated to God. We can do the most menial tasks in the home or any enterprise in the public square or marketplace and make it spiritual by doing it as unto Him, by doing it in Jesus' name.

Tucked away in a remote attic of a 19th-century Shaker home we discovered a beautiful built-in closet. Handcrafted drawers and cabinet doors, even after 100 years, display the superb skill of the craftsman who built them. Why would anyone go to such meticulous detail on a cupboard that would never be seen? Because the Shakers believed that everything made should be dedicated to God, should be pleasing to His eyes.

4. *Bezalel's gifts were described in specific terms.*

He was a goldsmith, silversmith, and bronzesmith (Exod. 35:32).

He was a stonecutter (v. 33).

He was a woodcarver (v. 33).

He was an engraver (v. 35).

He was a designer (v. 35).

He was an embroiderer (v. 35).

He was a weaver (v. 35).

And just in case something was overlooked, it's mentioned that he was skilled at performing in "every inventive work" (v. 33).

How did one man learn so many skills? Perhaps those skills were thrust on him in a flash by Almighty God. Zap! The day before, he couldn't cut mustard—today he can sculpt castles.

That could be. God can do that if He wants. He needs a Tabernacle builder, so He creates one.

But there's another scenario. It's more likely that Bezalel learned the basics of his skills the same way others of his day did—from his parents and grandparents.

At the right time, in the right place, God filled him with His Spirit. He allowed him to supervise the building of the Tabernacle. But long before that, some Hebrew grandma showed little Bezalel how to embroider. A Hebrew grandpa taught him the principles of woodcarving.

Perhaps the day will come for your grandchildren or ours when God will choose to use the skills we imparted to them for a specific project. Who knows for what future acts we're preparing them?

5. *The Lord stirred Bezalel's heart to teach* (v. 34).

Bezalel didn't desire fortune, followers, or fame. He wanted learners, apprentices. Don't you love this kind of dedicated, humble teacher? Every once in a while we sit under someone who has a passion, a drive, a compulsion to see that students progress, prosper, persevere, and above all, produce. That's the kind of man Bezalel was.

It would take more than one man to construct the Tabernacle. "No problem," we hear Bezalel shout. "I'll train them how to do it."

A strong penchant to pass on a legacy to your grandchildren might stem from a similar motivation. Perhaps the Lord has put it in your heart to teach them.

6. *Bezalel wasn't alone.* God supplied a team of coworkers and partners. There were others in whom "The LORD [had] put skill and understanding to know how to perform all the work in the construction of the sanctuary" (36:1).

Many hands, much sweat fashioned the Tabernacle. Hundreds of hours of work got the job done. But it wasn't a one-person accomplishment. Bezalel allowed others to do their parts as well. He recognized God's use of them in the final product.

Grandparents, too, must find the grace to acknowledge

that God has placed others around our grandchildren to impact their lives too. He can work through them, and sometimes in spite of them, to bring about His will and purpose for the child. Our prayer should be that God will bring positive influences, helpful relations, for their highest, spiritual good. We have partners in our grandparenting.

God allows people the privilege of helping in His work on earth. He uses prophets and priests, teachers and evangelists, missionaries and pastors. He also employs weavers and carvers and those skilled at "every inventive work."

A man or woman in Bible times who died and left no heirs was pitied. In families today, a loss is felt when the family name dies with the last namesake and there is no future generation to carry it on. Grandpa and Great-Grandpa and Great-Great-Grandpa would grieve to know the lineage stopped.

The loss of special skills should convict us too. They might be yours or your parent's or grandparent's.

Every trade, vocation, or handicraft that's lost shifts society to its lowest common denominator. We have to start all over to learn it.

You and I won't change the world, but we can attempt to stop the trend in one family.

7

The Power of Knowing Your Place

Grandparents are for telling you what it used to be like, but not too much.
—Charlie W. Shedd

We chatted with the couple at the table next to us as the restaurant's bay window magnified the setting sun on the Pacific Ocean. It was the end of the day, the end of the summer, and for the couple, the end of vacation.

"I miss the kids," the wife reported.

"We seldom get away by ourselves," the husband added. "But Lucy's folks came out from Texas and agreed to stay with the children so we'd have a relaxing five days."

"But I dread going back. Mom will have all the routines destroyed by now."

We probed for an explanation.

"Well," she said, "Richie will gripe because we don't buy him donuts every day like Grandpa did, and Bonnie will insist that she's old enough to stay up until 10 because Grandma said she was, and Tina will whine when we don't let her pick out the videos to rent."

"Yeah," the husband responded, "and Derrick will probably have another of those black T-shirts with some hideous rock group on the front that his grandpa bought for him.

"Sometimes," the wife said with a moan, "I don't know whether I'm happiest to see the folks come or to see them leave."

It's the other side of grandparenting. Grandparents can be a pain. Moms and dads need to have the support, not the carping or competition, of their children's grandparents in the tough task of parenting.

How can you spot a problem like this in your family? Watch for these phrases from either you or your adult children:

- "Mother, I really wish you wouldn't."

Which means, "Watch out, lady—you're about to exceed the limits."

- "Sorry, kids. Your *mother* won't let me do that."

Which means, "Your mother is the bad guy, and for the moment she has the upper hand. We can't do anything about it—yet."

- "Sure, honey—go ahead, but promise you won't tell your daddy I let you do it."

Which means, "Daddy's rules are flaky. It's all right to disobey them, providing you don't get caught."

- "I certainly think we could relax the rules just this one time for Grandma, couldn't we?"

Which means, "If you really loved me, you'd allow me this simple pleasure with my grandchildren since there's no telling how many more times I'll get to see them."

- "I'm sure your father must have *some* good reason for not letting you do that."

Which means, "Only a numbskull would enforce a restriction like that. But he'll get mad if I don't go along with it. So I'll play along—but I don't have to like it."

- "Honey, this is your mother's house. What can I say?"

Which means, "I know lots more about it than your mother does, but I'm prevented from spreading my great wisdom."

- "I don't know how my generation ever survived raising children without all the so-called experts around to tell us what to do."

Which means, "You don't have to read some book in order to know how to raise your kids. Common sense was good enough for my generation; it ought to work for yours."

You've heard these and have probably said some of them.

It's hard not to disagree on some aspect of how the grand-children are being raised.

Seven Areas of Possible Contention

Discipline

Grandparents are not the supreme court to which an appeal of injustice may be made. They are the friendly professors of family life who are on standby for advice to young and old—if asked.

God created mothers and fathers to give oversight to a flock of little people called "the kids." They are to love them, provide for them, protect them, and discipline them. The Bible says, "Children, be obedient to your parents in all things" (Col. 3:20). Notice it does not say, "Children, if your grandparents don't agree with your parents, you may choose which to obey."

We had our chance with our own kids. Today other schools of thought meld with ours—that of our adult child, a separate, thinking being; and that of our adult child's mate—another separate, thinking being. Our hope is they are wise enough to learn from our experiences and smart enough to avoid our mistakes.

But even when they don't learn the lessons well, even if they rebel against our counsel, even when they neglect God's guidance, they are still *the* mother and *the* father, the responsible party before God for the discipline of the children.

If we disagree over how to discipline the grandkids, here's what we can do:

● Publicly support our grandchildren's parents.

Eight-year-old Sam broke one of the game rules on his first day's visit: he did not pick up all the Lego blocks before bath time. The punishment, passed down by his parents beforehand—no Legos for two days.

"But, Grandma," Sam whines, "I'm only going to be here for four days. I wanted to show you my giant big truck stop."

Grandma replies, "I'm sorry too. Let's plan on playing with

those Legos on your last day here. You can show me the truck stop then."

"But you don't understand, Grandma. It's very hard to build. It would take most of the day. I don't think it's fair not getting to play with Legos just because I didn't pick them up."

Then you smile and say, "Sam, facing the consequences helps us learn how to do things right."

"But I thought Grandma's house would be fun," Sam pouts.

"Would you say making brownies is fun?" Grandma asks.

"The kind with the walnuts and the chocolate sauce?"

"Yep. Let's make some in the morning."

"Just you and me, Grandma?"

"Sure."

"All right."

- **Question discipline only when you can do it in private and when you have valid points to support your concern.**

Call your daughter and ask, "Dear, I wanted to check something out with you. I wonder if it would be all right with you if I allowed Junior to leave his Legos scattered in the den for a couple of days. He has so many projects to show me, and it doesn't bother me a bit. I just didn't want to do it without checking with you first."

- **Once you have appealed a disciplinary action, let the matter be settled.**

Don't bring it up again to your grandchildren, and don't bring it up again to their parents. Remember: they're trying to set standards they believe are best for this particular child. They're working for lifetime goals. We want peace for one visit, but they must live with the child every day.

Bedtime Hours

How strange it is! We forced our own kids to go to bed by 7:30, but we don't mind if the grandkids stay up until 10:00.

How *should* you respond?

Darling, blond-haired Trudy pleads, "Please, pretty please, Grandma—can't I just this once stay up to watch this show?"

You reply, "I'm sorry. Your bedtime is 8:30."

Trudy comes back with, "But, Grandma, lots of girls my age stay up until 10. I don't know why my mother won't let me stay up later."

To which you respond, "Well, Trudy, I've known your mother for years. She's a good mother. If she says 8:30, then that's it. But we'll do some fun things tomorrow."

"That's not fair," Trudy whines. "You're always on her side."

"That's because Grandma loves you and worries about you almost as much as your mother does."

"Almost as much?" Trudy sniffles.

"Well, precious, the Lord gave you only one mother and one father. I can tell you from experience: there's no one on this earth who can love you as much as they do."

A thoroughly modern grandma would have one other advantage. She could say, "Trudy, I'll set the timer and videotape that program so you can watch it in the morning."

Food and Nutrition

Your daughter-in-law insists that your grandchildren should not have any white sugar, white flour, white bread, or salt. Somehow you survived to a lively age not worrying about any of those things. So when the grandkids come over, what do you feed them? Donuts. Fruit Loops. French fries. Hot dogs on white buns. Sugary red Kool-Aid. And that's just for breakfast!

Or maybe it's the daughter-in-law who feeds them that way and you're the health-conscious one. Either way, there's conflict.

The easiest way to deal with this problem is to major on feeding your grandchildren moderate amounts of healthful food—few moms complain about that.

If you know specific foods that their parents forbid, honor that choice. If you have an important reason to feed them something different, call your grandchild's parents ahead of time and ask permission.

"Honey, there's a new little bakery in the mall. Is it OK to take Cindy there for some tea and sweets this afternoon?" This leaves Mom still in charge of nutrition. And you have proved that you're not trying to circumvent her.

Television

At 11 o'clock every weekday morning you watch a one-hour soap opera. So when Lorie comes to stay, you think nothing of flipping on the set. Besides, today you'll find out if Sid is going to propose to Clarita, or will he let her raise the baby alone? And if he proposes, will Lulu have him arrested for breaking and entering? Not only that, will Rodney be caught making passes at both Lulu and her sister, Jasmine?

So when your daughter drops off Lorie, she informs you, "Don't let her watch any of your horrible soap operas."

This can go either way, of course.

Lorie flips on some late-night show about a lady dope dealer who gets raped and then goes on a rampage with a butcher knife. When you tell her, "Turn that off," she replies, "But my folks always let me watch this program."

How to settle the dilemma? One solution is to keep so busy with other activities that no one has any time to watch TV at all. Radical? Sure. But TV can wait. Don't waste valuable top-quality time with a soon-to-be-grown grandchild mesmerized before a noisy, demanding box.

The Amount and Kinds of Gifts

On Alex's fifth birthday, Grandpa bought him a fancy set of cap pistols, complete with imitation leather holsters and fake plastic bullets in the belt.

On Alex's 10th birthday, Grandpa provided him with a deluxe Daisy BB gun and a three-pound box of BBs.

On Alex's 15th birthday, Grandpa bought him a Winchester '94 carbine, complete with scabbard, targets, and bullets.

What do these three events have in common? Each of these gifts made Alex's mother furious. She did not want her son owning guns, knives, or bows and arrows. She would not even allow Alex to play with toy soldiers, tanks, or jet bombers.

"Grandpa knows that I don't approve," she fumes.

"She's trying to make a sissy out of that boy," he thunders back.

As well-meaning as Grandpa might be, he's creating a wedge between himself and his daughter-in-law and also between Alex and his mother. He has set himself up as the "good guy" and Mom as the "bad guy." No present is worth that.

Conversations in Front of the Children

A hideous rape and murder takes place in the same city where your daughter lives. When you stop by for a visit, she wants to talk about the crime. As she begins to give you the grisly details, you notice your grandchildren playing in the corner of the room.

"Uh, maybe we should talk about this some other time," you suggest, raising your eyebrows toward the children.

"Oh, they never pay attention to what we're talking about," your daughter replies, then launches into another description of the crime as you wince.

Your daughter, noticing your obvious discomfort, throws up her hands in disgust. "Mother, this has really bothered me. I don't know why you just can't hear me out."

Conflict. Should kids hear about murders and rapes? Should the conversations in front of them ever turn to prostitution, homosexuality, adultery? Should they hear about demons, ghosts, and Satan worship? Should they enter into conversations about auto accidents, bloody bodies, and death? Are there topics that are off limits for kids? If so, what are they?

Have you ever asked your grandchildren's parents what subjects they would rather you didn't talk about in front of the kids? Sounds as if that would be a good place to start.

Spiritual Teaching and Growth

Many Christian grandparents endure the pain of knowing their very own grandchildren don't get spiritual teaching.

Freda knows that agony. Her grandson, Nick, came to visit last July. "How's the youth group at church?" Freda asked the seventh-grader.

"I don't go, Grandma."

"What? How come?"

"It's too boring. My folks said I don't have to if I don't want to."

"And church?"

"Nah. Lots of Sundays there are dirt bike races. I need to compete if I'm ever going to get really good."

At least you know he had some exposure when he was younger. Others have none at all.

Grandparents may have little inroad into what happens in their grandchild's home. But you can set a different pattern and tone in your own home. If you say grace before every meal, even when out in public, don't stop because of the grandkids. If you read a Bible passage every morning during breakfast, then continue the practice no matter who's sitting at the table with you. If your habit is going to Sunday School and church, then insist that all who are in your home do the same.

When Nick or his parents complain, just smile and say, "Oh, now—that's just the way I am. You know grandmas—they get set in their ways."

Why Grandparents and Their Children Differ About Raising Kids

There seem to be four prime causes for parenting conflicts. *Sometimes biblical principles are involved.*

Ned and Nadine couldn't believe that their son and his wife would give Penny permission to go on a two-week camping trip with her boyfriend—just the two of them. For Ned and Nadine, it's not merely a social custom or cultural issue.

Ned and Nadine couldn't condone the behavior, no matter how much they wanted to support Penny's parents. It violated scriptural warnings about sex and single girls. They couldn't find an exception for compromise. They tried to be sensitive to feelings, compassionate with their judgment, and loving with their reprimand, but they felt they had to take a stand and make their feelings known. And accept the results.

Ned and Nadine cringe about other things too. When they

raised their son they had strict rules about what kinds of movies he would be allowed to watch. But first Penny, then her sister, Abby, were allowed to attend movies Ned and Nadine never would have approved. They have grieved over what they consider unwise privileges—and they might be right. But this is not a clear-cut biblical issue. Ned and Nadine determined that they would bite their tongues on subjects like this unless they were asked. And they never have been asked.

Grandparents aren't always aware of all the variables to be considered in parents' decisions.

Mazie's son and daughter-in-law opted to home-school the grandchildren. But the whole idea, as far as Mazie could see, robbed the kids of a classroom experience with other children. As she drove to the grocery, she would pass the grade school in her town and see the children playing in the school yard. Half of the teachers in this school attended Mazie's church. She personally knew of their strong faith and commitment to the Lord and to children. She couldn't reconcile the fact of her own grandchildren stuck at home with their mother all day long.

"All the rest of us survived public schools," she muttered to herself.

But Mazie didn't live on the south side of Chicago where any moment she could expect to hear shots fired or sirens blaring. She didn't have to deal with dope dealers hanging around the playgrounds of the nearby elementary school.

Mazie didn't have all the facts. These parents were doing everything they could to provide the best education environment possible for their kids.

Your children may not choose to parent exactly the way you did.

A natural tendency is to assume our children will raise their own children exactly as we raised them. We admit we may have made a mistake or two, but for the most part, we passed muster as mother and father. We expect our kids to do the same.

We raised our boys on powdered milk—why do the grandkids drink whole milk?

We ironed the kids' clothes, and they looked crisp and clean for school every day. Why are the grandkids wearing wrinkled t-shirts to school?

I packed my kids' lunches.

No decent girl ever had her ears pierced.

What kind of father would let his kid get a tattoo?

Differences based on culture, eras, fads, preferences.

Worry if they aren't being loved. Pray if they have no spiritual nurture. Take action if they're being abused. But try to relax and let go of your concerns about the changing tide of methods, styles, and theories.

Power struggles are hard to detect and difficult to admit.

Why does that classic friction arise between wife and mother-in-law? Because of a struggle to control the life of one man. When the grandchildren arrive, they're fuel for smoldering fire. Whose will is going to prevail?

Grandma shows up with an oversized box of bubble gum. The kids are charmed, but their mother is not. "You know I don't like them to chew that sugary stuff," she stews behind their backs.

On one hand, Grandma could have brought them a basket of fresh fruit, and the kids would have been happy. On the other hand, their mother allows some gum now and then, with no undue damage to their teeth. But the gum isn't really what this is about. It's about control.

Grandma defies. Mother snits. The turf wars rage.

Wise grandparents know the difference between actions that can be interpreted as assaults on authority and true acts of love.

Eight Things You Can Do in One Visit to Support Your Grandchildren's Parents

1. Within three minutes of walking through the front door, sincerely compliment your grandchild's parents. Establish the fact that your visit is not meant to be a formal inspection.

2. Ask your grandchild's mother for her advice on a parenting problem one of your friend's faces.

Patsy's best friend's daughter struggled with how to cope with a strong-willed three-year-old. Patsy asked her own daughter if she had any suggestions. Patsy admitted she was not a parenting expert and established a new rapport with her daughter.

3. Before you visit, call. Tell them you would like to bring a present to the kids. Ask them if there's anything they would suggest. That way there's no surprises to explain. If they have a preference, you'll please the parents as well as the child. If they tell you anything will do, then they have no basis for complaint. And you've credited their decisions as of primary importance in the children's parenting.

4. Find a project that involves you and the grandkids, and jump right into it. Sit down and read them a book. Work on a puzzle. Play a board game. Review the baseball card collection. Have a pretend tea party with dolls. This gives mother a breather, and she doesn't have to worry about entertaining you or watching out for the children.

5. If your visit is by invitation to a special event, volunteer for any job to help out.

Repeat your offer if they first say, "No, thanks—we've got everything under control." Then drop it. This is their event, and they're in charge. Accept a subordinate position.

6. If it's polite to do so, defer any home leadership roles that are thrust upon you.

Your daughter says, "Well, Dad, I guess you always carve the Thanksgiving turkey," and hands you the knife. Just hand the knife on down to your son-in-law and say, so the kids can hear, "Oh, I'm sure Jim can do it as well as I can."

7. Eliminate words and phrases with double meanings.

If little Gwen's blouse has dried mustard stains on it, don't say in a loud voice for her mother to hear, "Why, Gwen, I thought for a minute you had one of those new tie-dyed blouses. But, you know, honey, you'd look cute no matter what old thing you wore."

8. Hug the whole family, not just the kids. Demonstrate to the grandchildren that your love is the same for them and

their parents. Show that you're not trying to build a special coalition that bypasses the middle generation. It's not you and the grandkids against the parents.

When your children were small, chances are you had an opportunity to sit in the crowd and watch them perform. You were there at your daughter's piano recitals when she froze up and didn't remember what to do next. You were there when your son struck out in the ninth inning of the big game.

You sat with pride and amazement when your girl spoke at the commencement address. You stood tall and proud as your son received the medal of courage from his commanding officer. Whether they succeeded or failed, you were ready to support, encourage, and console. You were on their side.

Now that your children are grown, some things don't change. They succeed. They fail. They struggle with their own strengths and weaknesses.

Some of those failures will come in parenting. We can still be on their side, to encourage, to support, to console. We're not to demand a perfection from them we couldn't achieve ourselves.

Grandchildren are resilient. Toss them into a cauldron of inexperienced parents, great love, personal struggles, forgiveness, spiritual sensitivity, a touch of pain and sorrow, lots of laughs, and supportive grandparents—and it's amazing how well they turn out, no matter what the parenting system.

8

The Power of Being There If Your Grandchildren's Parents Divorce

When a child is born, so are grandmothers.
—Judith Levy

Christian grandparents raise Christian children who find Christian mates and produce Christian grandchildren. Then the whole family lives happily ever after until the day the Lord returns. Right? We wish!

We all hope that story is true for our family, and we all pray it will be that way. But it isn't always.

Christian grandparents sometimes raise children who never know the Lord. Christian children sometimes marry unbelievers. And, sadly, even Christian sons and daughters married to Christian mates don't always know how to do marriage.

The result, so evident in our world today, is an epidemic of divorce. We hope you don't need this chapter, but lots of folks will.

Every person is accountable to God for his or her own sins. "Behold, all souls are Mine; the soul of the father as well as the soul of the son is Mine. The soul who sins will die" (Ezek. 18:4). Yet children pay plenty for their parents' sins.

Paula married Ted, and in nine years they produced five children and too many unresolved differences to name. Paula left the four boys and one girl with Ted one Friday night and never returned.

But since the marriage had been stormy, they both said, "Good riddance." After all, they had to do what was best for them.

Paula earned her living by singing in cheap bars and drank cheaper whiskey until, 10 years and three husbands later, she dried out and tried one more attempt at marriage. She still struggles to hold it together as she raises a new family.

Ted fought to raise the kids in a two-room house in Salt Lake City. Live-in girlfriends came and went as the kids grew up with no notion of stable family.

All the kids married right out of high school. Ted then talked his best friend's wife into deserting her husband to marry him. This left the best friend's four teenage daughters in a single-parent home. But, after all, the parents had to do what was right for them.

Among Ted and Paula's five children there have been seven divorces and countless live-ins. Of Ted's stepdaughters, two have already divorced. They had to, of course, for their own good.

Ted and Paula have contributed, all or in part, to umpteen broken relationships and a barrage of confusing, crippling liaisons. And the cycle keeps going and going and going.

Ted and Paula can claim, "We're not the only ones." They're right, of course. You could probably top this chronology with an account of someone you know. This scenario is not that unusual anymore. We suffer a social and family quagmire of noncommitment.

Our role as grandparents is to help minimize the damage anyway we can. God's grace pours out on hurting families who deal with the tragedy of estrangement. Perhaps your own grandchildren are caught in the wreckage. God's grace is freely given to guilty sinners in defiance of what they deserve. Part of our spiritual legacy can be extending God's grace into whatever murky mess surrounds us and our grandchildren.

Ten Important Points to Remember

1. **Most kids love both Mommy and Daddy, no matter who seems to be the guilty party.**

The love of one's parents is a God-given affection. At times it defies logic.

Genevieve and her two girls took the bus to Denver to visit her sister. When they returned two days early, she found that her husband, George, had tangled with a college girl in Genevieve's brief absence. The girl's belongings scattered the house. Divorce proceedings exposed that George had had others, too, through the years. Since then, George has had a steady stream of lady friends and a wife or two. His daughters, now in their teens, seldom see him. They never even get a note at birthdays or Christmas.

However, they still miss their dad. They write him long letters that are often returned. They love their father, and no amount of discussion will change that. Their love is not based on rational thought or feeling. It is based on a decision of their will. They choose to offer their father natural affection.

Genevieve's parents don't try to set the girls straight about their errant parent. Instead, they rejoice that the girls re-tained a capacity to love in spite of what they have gone through. They're thankful that the father didn't kill their love. That might be his only link to turning around his life.

Genevieve's parents don't lie about George's character or his behavior. They don't tell the girls they think he's a won-derful father, "when he's acting like a jerk."

"But they've got to know that love isn't something that's earned only by good behavior. If God loved us that way, who would ever be loved?"

"God demonstrates His own love toward us, in that while we were yet sinners, Christ died for us" (Rom. 5:8).

2. Your in-law may assume that you're on the side of your child and are therefore a potential enemy.

It's difficult to remain neutral in domestic fights. Separa-tion or divorce often forces us to choose sides.

One of our society's biggest lies is that divorce affects only two principal parties: the husband and the wife. At least two other groups suffer, too, for years down the road—the chil-dren and the grandparents.

So the divorce is final and the lines are drawn. Where do you fit? Most often on the side of your child. You'll be related to your child for the rest of your life.

But some of the family is not on your side of the line anymore. Your former son-in-law or daughter-in-law, his or her parents, and maybe even your own grandchildren stand in the opposite corner.

The only thing you can do other than pray is to try to soften the division. Fights fizzle more quickly when one side refuses to swing. Be sensitive to speak the truth without becoming a combatant. Paul said, "If possible, so far as it depends on you, be at peace with all men" (Rom. 12:18).

Six months after their son divorced, the Woodakers felt alienated from Sylvia and the girls. They weren't sure if they were still welcome. They felt awkward about initiating visits, because the girls always asked about their father, and they felt Sylvia's apprehension about their motivation for the visit.

Before the divorce, the Woodakers had a habit of popping in on the grandkids every other week and calling them in between. But now they're considering cutting back. "Perhaps we should limit our contacts to holidays."

Finally, they called Sylvia and confessed, "We want to be the best grandparents we can for the girls. What would be most helpful to you?"

Sylvia insisted they continue the familiar routine. "The girls need you more than ever."

But now it was being done because Sylvia requested it. She was recognized as the decision maker. And now she could welcome the girls' grandparents without being threatened.

3. Whether you're allowed to see your grandchildren depends upon the parent with custody.

One of the biggest fears of grandparents is that they'll lose all contact with their grandchildren. The judge rarely assures grandparents' visiting rights.

Gene and Norma watched their dreams for Myles unravel. Raised in a Christian home, young Myles rebelled against his parents, authority, school, and society. At age 17 his pregnant girlfriend and he decided to marry.

A few months after Joey was born, Myles was fired from his day-labor job for drunkenness. The three came to live with Gene and Norma. When Myles decided to join the Marines, the three of them moved off to Georgia. Gene and Norma didn't hear much from Myles or Kimberly for two years. Then Kimberly wrote a short note that she was expecting another baby.

Gene and Norma planned a trip to Georgia to see the new baby, but Kimberly quickly responded, "Don't come. Myles is in the brig and doesn't want to see you."

After Sebastian was born, Myles was given a dishonorable discharge from the Marines because of possession of drugs. Kimberly filed for divorce. Both sides bitterly tried to prove the other an unfit parent.

Kimberly and the kids, and then Myles, moved back to the hometown after the divorce. The court ruled that Kim had custody, but Myles could have the children two weekends a month.

However, neither parent paid much attention to the kids. They were batted around as pawns for leverage. Myles seldom took his turn, and Kimberly allowed Gene and Norma to pick up Joey and Sebastian for those two weekends a month. So Norma washes the children's filthy clothes and gives them overdue baths. She's trained them to brush their teeth, eat good food, and attend Sunday School.

Gene and Norma are concerned for their grandchildren's welfare. They would gladly take care of the children permanently. When they mentioned this to Kimberly, she got incensed and wouldn't bring the boys at all for six months.

Gene and Norma sigh in despair, "Neither of the parents is responsible enough to have those little guys, but we can't do one thing about it. We just watch, worry, and pray."

For now, their part is to be an occasional island of calm in the tempestuous lives of their grandsons.

4. Each side will have their explanation of why the marriage failed. Make an effort to understand them both.

You can give advice and intercede through prayer, but no

one can live someone else's marriage. The partners make their own choices, and we seldom hear the entire story of how and why a marriage ended. People manage the information they release as tightly as a totalitarian dictator. You hear what they want you to hear, and the spin usually supports the one doing the talking.

Beatrice was shocked when her daughter, Lucy, called to say she left Dave. She said she caught him having an affair with a woman at work. Since Beatrice had never heard any hint of anything wrong in the marriage, she was quick to take Lucy's side.

But finally, after a clumsy meeting in a supermarket aisle, Beatrice had a chance to hear Dave's side. "Did you know," he said, "that she forced me to sleep on the sofa for the last two and half years?"

No, she had not known. But now she knew there was more to the story.

The potential for complexity in any relationship is astounding. The webs of misunderstanding, the deceit, the barriers we build prove our need for God. He works through our tangled messes to instruct us on the next step. He heals aching hearts.

5. There's such a thing as a wronged party. Sometimes there's only one person to blame, and perhaps that one person is your son or daughter.

It may not be a two-way street. One person can break up a marriage no matter how hard the other tries to save it.

After years of what seems to be a happy marriage, one of the partners announces, "I need some time to myself," and moves to Alaska.

That's it. No warnings. No complaints. No reasons. Just gone.

In Matt. 19:3-9 Jesus says that adultery is so harmful that it can rip apart the marriage bond. If one of the marriage partners has committed adultery, the other is certainly wronged.

Sin is not justified by stating how miserable a person was before he or she committed it. If one of the divorcing parties has sinned, repentance is due. All the love and concern you show him or her cannot overlook this process. But knowing the reasons helps us understand.

6. Unless the children are abandoned by both parents, your role is not to be a substitute mother or father but to be the very best grandparent possible.

In the child's mind, he or she has a mother and father already no matter how little he or she might see them. This frees you to fulfill only one role—that of grandparent. The kids need to see through you that some relationships never change. Some people can be counted on.

Grandparents are supposed to act like a grandma and grandpa. When Portia calls and says, "Grandma, I'm almost 12. Don't you think I'm old enough to wear makeup?" you can say, "Oh, my, honey—that's something a girl and her mother ought to decide. Whatever you two come up with will be fine with me."

You don't need to make mother-like decisions, even when there are subtle temptations to do so.

7. Divorce does not indicate that the mother or father are inadequate parents.

Even the parent responsible for destroying the marriage does not forfeit his or her parenting rights. A person can be a terrible spouse and still love his or her children dearly.

When you see your grandchildren of divorce, find something to compliment—their clothes, behavior, or manners. Their custodial parent will hear of it, and the implied message is "Hang in there—you're doing a good job at parenting.

8. Divorce does not invalidate other good qualities, skills, and achievements.

Divorce does not mean that the parents are incapable of doing any good. If your son-in-law was a wonderful lawyer before the divorce, he probably still is. If you didn't hesitate to recommend him to your friends then, don't change your mind now.

If you viewed your child and his or her mate as perfect in every way, then divorce will change your image. They are humans who flourish or fall, who obey or disobey, who shine or muck it up.

You can still enjoy your daughter's prominence at the university or your son-in-law's latest book. And you can be proud of those achievements in front of the grandchildren.

Charlotte had always been a nurse at heart. She traveled the circuit of the family, tending to the sick and infirm. She was the one who showed up with meals, ran to the pharmacy to fill a prescription, and did all the wash when anyone was down on his back. She would sit beside the bed in the hospital all night and manage to be fresh and chipper the next morning.

Thirteen years ago Charlotte divorced Lyle and Andrea Anderson's son, Vince, and within weeks she married a shoe store owner. The Andersons have seen her only a few times since then. Last September Lyle was in a serious car wreck. His wife, Andrea, stuck by his side for two weeks. Her only breaks came when Charlotte came to sit with him in the evenings.

When Lyle no longer lingered on the critical list, Andrea was gratified to find that Charlotte had cleaned the house and left the freezer stocked with casseroles. Whatever other faults Charlotte has, her ability to show mercy and come alongside with practical helps has not dimmed.

9. Your model of marriage could provide essential family stability.

If the challenge has been great, if you survived a major marital crisis, there's more reason to rejoice. Committed couples combat enemies within and without. Those who endure have a tale to tell to the next generation.

When the family unit is strong, a grandparent's lifelong marriage establishes one more cornerstone in showing grandchildren what a stable relationship looks like. But when chronic divorce or live-in habits hit a home, one secure covenant relationship example becomes critical for evidence that it can be done. It *is* possible to do it right.

Because so much revolves around this relationship, we must practice the fine art of showing appropriate affection to our mates in front of the grandkids. We can illustrate for them what it means to love. Little eyes are watching, and we have another reason to persevere, to make it work.

For instance, their parents, now divorced, rail at each other all the time. They never forgive. How will they ever witness forgiveness in action?

Grandma Kathryn admitted to her grandkids, "I was so angry with your grandpa when he went out and bought that speed boat."

Robbie's eyes get big. "What did you do, Grandma?"

"I said a bunch of stupid things. Then I cried, we hugged, and we made up."

"You didn't stay mad?"

"Nah, that boat wasn't worth coming between me and your grandpa."

"Did he take the boat back?"

"Well, I think he would have. But I got so I like the boat. It's a lot nicer than the other one we had. And Grandpa promised he'd never buy another boat without talking it over with me first."

Kathryn wouldn't have bothered with sharing that scene with Robbie, except she felt he needed to know his grandparents worked through their troubles and still loved each other when they got upset. She opened up this part of their lives for his inspection.

10. Grandchildren whose parents are divorced may need more intense attention than your other grandchildren, but be careful not to neglect the others.

Another reason it's so hard for grandparents to become mother and father to some of their grandchildren is that the others still need them to remain Grandma and Grandpa.

You don't need a stopwatch to clock the time you spend with individual grandchildren to assure equal time for all. In different seasons, different ages, different circumstances, individual grandchildren need more attention than others.

But those coping with divorce shouldn't receive greater conspicuous rewards.

"I always resented my cousin Christy," Danny told us. "Her

folks were divorced, so every Christmas Grandma gave her
the biggest presents. 'She needs it more than you others,' I
was told. It was Christy who got to go on vacation with
Grandma. Christy got Grandma's car when she turned 16.
Christy lived with Grandma when she got out of college. I
can actually remember thinking while growing up, 'Boy, I
wish *my* folks were divorced.'"

Tough Situations in Which
Your Guidance Is Especially Needed

There are at least three areas in which your grandchildren
will be looking for your example.

Forgiveness

What do we do when grandchildren become bitter toward
a parent? This is more common when parents refuse to forgive each other.

Forgiveness is as Christian as good deeds. It affects our relationships with God. Jesus said, "If you forgive others for
their transgressions, your heavenly Father will also forgive
you. But if you do not forgive others, then your Father will
not forgive your transgressions" (Matt. 6:14-15).

But to forgive is never simple, never easy, and not much
fun. To replace pride and fury with warm, fuzzy feelings for a
person who hurt us or hurt someone we love is a miracle to
the max. To forgive requires a major brain overhaul.

The responsibility of being a grandparent who wants to
leave a spiritual legacy is to show your grandchildren how you
forgive. When they see you do it, they're more likely to
chance it for themselves.

Remarriage

The crisis for grandkids intensifies when Mom or Dad re-
marries. This often doubles the misery of divorce. The children are forced to deal with parent substitutes and more siblings. They must absorb the shock of different aunts and
uncles and cousins and, yes, grandparents. They may suddenly
feel like an outsider looking through a double-pane window
into their own home. Where do they fit now?

And where do *you* fit? As you face adjustments in the newly formed family structure, it's a challenge to avoid becoming part of the problem. Deal with the awkwardness or disappointments by grasping the long run of relationships and life. This, too, will pass.

Ask yourself, *What kind of attitude do my grandchildren need from me to help them get beyond the present situation?* Demonstrate compassion and mercy that will wear well on your grandchildren for years to come.

The Channels of Communication

Your former daughter-in-law moves the children to Maine. You have no idea when you'll see them again. What can you do?

First, communicate. Write, phone, send tapes—whatever you're allowed. The children are the victims. Don't withhold your loving attention because of their parent's choices. Suggestions given in earlier chapters about long-distance grandparenting become critical now.

If you're told to stop communicating so often with your grandchildren, try to stay within the limits the parent suggests. But for the children's sake, don't lose contact. Even letters that are never answered can express love. Make sure your correspondence doesn't dig into old wounds.

Second, pray. Those grandchildren taken from your presence might need your prayers most of all. Pray for their safety, their maturity, their self-image, their relationships, and their salvation.

Divorce is like a wrecked ship. The voyage ends on a shattered beach. The dream of a united, peaceful landing is dashed to bits.

But it doesn't mean that the whole family drowns. Grandma and Grandpa can still be there. Always the same. Always available for counsel. Ready with a life jacket and a steady relationship.

Grandparents have a legacy to pass on to struggling grandchildren for the sake of a marooned family.

9

The Power of Sharing Spiritual Truth

As a grandparent seeking to strengthen a grandchild's devotional life, you should build on the parents' foundation as much as possible.
—Eric Wiggin

Travis could hardly wait.

"I always do fun things at my grandma and grandpa's house," he told his friends.

This visit was no exception. A couple of days later, he reported to his neighborhood gang. "We went to Burger Den, and I had a jumbo bacon cheeseburger. Then we stopped at the Ice Cream Palace. I had two scoops of double fudge. Next we went to the toy store. My grandpa bought me some Star Wars Legos. On our way back to their house we stopped by the video store. I got to pick out the movie."

Travis had a good time, but there's more to the story. Travis eats at the Burger Den at least once a week. He always orders a jumbo bacon cheeseburger. There's an Ice Cream Palace about a block away from his house—he's one of their regular customers. The evening was just a repeat of his normal routines. Grandma and Grandpa could have been more creative.

We've heard about the "songs and stories learned at your grandma's knee." We learned about everything from Mother

Goose to Aesop's Fables, Elizabeth Barrett Browning to Shakespeare, Noah's ark to the fiery furnace from our grandparents. Where has that kind of grandparent gone?

"Kids don't want to sit still and listen anymore," we hear grandparents complain. This is probably true, but kids don't like to brush their teeth either. Yet grandparents make them brush. Kids need grandparents to teach them. They need a mentoring grandparent to teach and reinforce spiritual truth.

What is a grandparent's spiritual responsibility? Deut. 4:9 says,

> Give heed to yourself and keep your soul diligently, so that you do not forget the things which your eyes have seen and they do not depart from your heart all the days of your life; but make them known to your sons and your grandsons.

And again, Deut. 6:1-2:

> Now this is the commandment, the statutes and the judgments which the LORD your God has commanded me to teach you, that you might do them in the land where you are going over to posses it, so that you and your son and your grandson might fear the LORD your God, to keep all His statutes and His commandments, which I command you, all the days of your life, and that your days may be prolonged.

The Bible doesn't tell us that the Church is to be the primary teacher of the faith to the next generation. Rather, it exhorts parents and grandparents to be prime instructors of spiritual education.

The first verse warns grandparents: *Pay strict attention to your own spiritual life.* Unless we're alert in prayer and practice, we can blow our spiritual credentials. But these disciplines can be reignited as we relive them with and through our grandchildren.

The second passage pleads: *Obey the Word of God.* By example, we encourage our children and grandchildren to do the same.

Conveying Spiritual Values to Your Grandkids

Don't

- place a pulpit in the living room and line up the grandkids to hear a sermon
- relegate spiritual discussions to Sundays only
- discuss theological differences, church fights, and personality conflicts
- picture God holding a hammer ready to smash children who disobey
- criticize other churches and denominations
- put down the spiritual life (or lack of it) of their parents
- make cultural customs more important than biblical truth
- make your love dependent upon their spiritual progress
- expect to excite them with spiritual truth using the same methods that were used on you years ago
- unload all your biblical knowledge in one sitting

Instead, try the following:

Whenever you talk of the past, include spiritual events as well. "Grandpa, where were you during the flood?" Heather asks.

"Noah's flood?"

Heather politely laughs. "No, the big flood of '49. We studied it in school last week."

"I was right here in River City."

"Well, what happened?"

"I remember it was on a Sunday. It had been raining for days," Grandpa explains. "We were scheduled to go down to the river for a baptism service. But the storm hit, and the river busted its banks. Mortimer Mackintosh was going to be baptized, and no one wanted to miss that."

Heather interrupts. "Who was Mortimer Mackintosh?"

"He owned the newspaper in River City for years, and most of that time he wrote scathing columns that ripped apart nearly every minister, church, and Christian in town. Then one Sunday morning he showed up at the pastor's door before church began. He claimed he had to find out the truth about religion and God once and for all. Well, by the 11 o'clock service he realized his sinful condition and walked down the aisle and gave his heart to the Lord."

"Did he stop writing those bad things about Christians?"

"He sure did. And he invited everyone in town to his baptism. But the floods came, and we couldn't get near the river. Folks said it was a sign of the devil's wrath because he didn't want Mortimer Mackintosh getting saved."

"Wow! Did he ever get baptized?"

"Oh, yes. The water rushed down First Street right in front of the church. There used to be a baseball field across the street in the lower end of the lot, and the water stood about four feet at home plate. So the preacher marched old Mortimer Mackintosh right into the floodwaters. He got baptized then and there. Mortimer bragged for years how the Lord made it so easy for him by bringing the river right to the front door of the church!"

Openly demonstrate your spiritual priority by faithful devotions. Grandma's Bible is kept on the end table next to her recliner in the living room. It usually sits there next to the television remote control and the *TV Guide*.

But the *TV Guide* seldom gets opened. It's a gift subscription from a distant relative. The remote control has no batteries and has never been used—Grandma never figured out how it works. But the Bible? The golden gilding has long since worn off, and the leather is cracked. The pages are marked and tattered, and cellophane tape holds much of it together.

It doesn't take six-year-old Kelsey long to discover which item is most important to her grandma. When we ask her to tell us the difference between mommies and grandmas, she says, "Moms don't like to start the day without drinking some coffee first. Grandmas read their Bible."

"My grandma gets on her knees to pray," Gregory reported to us. "Sometimes I hear her pray for me. But sometimes I'm so good she doesn't have to pray much at all."

Remember two things about what you demonstrate in front of your grandkids:

- Make it sincere. Don't invent some phony behavior just when the grandkids come over.
- Make it consistent. Whether they come to see you on Sunday or Tuesday, it should be the same. If you pray before meals at home, make sure you do the same when you take them out to the restaurant or eat a hamburger on the way home from the park. If they travel with you on vacation, demonstrate that you keep your same Bible reading schedule even then.

Do your grandkids know your personal testimony of how you came to the Lord?

Eight-year-old Brian drew us a picture of his family. There was the typical house and tree, three big stick figures and four little ones, and a stick dog. In the right-hand corner, above the clouds and the birds, was one more stick figure.

"Who are the people in the picture?" we asked.

"That's my mom and my dad, my Grandma Jewel, my three sisters, and Buster, my dog."

"Well, how about up there in the clouds?" we prodded.

"That's my Grandpa Verne. He's in heaven, you know."

"Oh," we asked, "was he a Christian?"

"Yes," Brian smiled. "Grandpa told me that he was 12 years old and working one summer for a Christian neighbor who told him about Jesus after supper on the Fourth of July."

"You sure know a lot about your grandfather," we said.

Brian nodded. "Yeah, we were best friends."

And somewhere up there, Grandpa Verne is smiling.

In sharing your testimony, tell them what a difference knowing Christ has made in your life. Were certain fears eased? Habits conquered? Relationships healed? Direction for life received? Make sure they understand exactly what changed.

Take them to Sunday School and church with you. Although Marion had visited her grandchildren in Georgia often, this was their first trip to visit her in Seattle. So the Sunday before they arrived, Marion visited the Sunday School rooms where her two granddaughters would attend. She chatted with their teachers, mentioned the girls would be coming, and took a good look at the classroom. As she was visiting, she noticed one of the younger ladies in her Bible study bringing in her daughter. Marion set up a time for her granddaughters to play with the friend's little girl.

During the week, Grandma Marion told the girls about their classrooms and what kinds of things they would do at Sunday School. By playing with the other little girl, she insured that they would know at least one other student in class.

When Sunday came, the girls were eager to go and delighted to have the teacher greet them by name. They quickly felt at home in the church.

Scenes like this don't just happen. Grandma prepared the way.

Spend time in a top-quality Christian bookstore to survey the latest materials available for their ages. Don't rely on what you liked as a child or what you used with your own children. The bookstore will have puzzles, games, videos, study booklets, picture books, adventure novels, and stacks full of creative material to present spiritual insights.

Here are a few helps for buying good books for your grandchild:

- Find something for each child to call his or her own (even if the book is to be left at your house).
- Don't guess at what age-group a book is aimed. Ask a clerk at the store.
- Look for stories that will last and be relevant for years to come.
- Make sure the spiritual message comes across clearly and that it's scriptural. If you can't easily figure out the message of a book, chances are that your grandchild won't be able to either.
- Take the grandchildren with you to the Christian bookstore. It will save time and trouble if you select two or three options from which they can choose.

Use the holidays to reinforce spiritual truth. Thanksgiving cards can display more than dancing turkeys, and Christmas cards should emphasize the birth of Jesus. Choose Easter cards that glorify a risen Savior.

But sending a religious card is not enough. Include a personal note of encouragement, affirmation, and love.

- "Collin, I was just thanking the Lord the other day for what a wonderful grandson I have. You're one of the people He uses to make my life so special. Thanks for being you. Love, Grandpa."
- "Julia, I just love Christmas, don't you? Especially the songs and the decorated tree and the presents. And to think the greatest present of all was when God sent His only Son, Jesus, to be our Savior. It's His birthday, and we get all the presents. Wow—we have a great God, don't we? Love, Grandma."
- "Wesley, isn't Easter a fun time? On Good Friday we're all sad remembering that Jesus had to die for us. But on Easter Jesus rose from the dead! It just goes to show how powerful and loving our God is. Love, Grandma."
- "I can't believe it—Clarissa is 10 years old! I'm sure glad the Lord allowed me to be your granddad. Have a great birthday, and remember: I'm going to keep right on praying for you no matter how big you get. Love, Granddad."

If your grandchildren spend the holidays with you, you can do even more. You could have some appropriate scriptures to read, prayers to offer, and times to reflect on God's goodness and provision over the years.

Give some presents with a spiritual purpose, but include fun gifts as well. Don't get the reputation of "Grandma never gives me anything fun." Buy the best children's study Bible on the market *and* a top-quality Little League baseball bat. Give a cassette tape of delightful Christian tunes for children and that adorable teddy bear you saw at the department store.

Demonstrate that you care about all areas of their lives. One grandmother reported that she used gift-giving as a special time of correspondence with the grandchildren. In each letter she talks about the true meaning of the holiday. But she also includes a toy catalog. Then she writes, "Honey, I've marked some toys that Grandma wants to buy you, but I just can't make up my mind. How about you picking your favorite five from the ones I marked in red?"

Her grandkids spend days making and remaking their list from Grandma's catalog. Then they write back to her with the results. The kids learn two clear facts about Grandma: she always talks about the Lord, and she likes having fun too.

Read to them. Grandparents can never read too often to their grandkids. Never. Read Bible stories, missionary stories, adventure stories. Read lessons from science and nature, biographies of famous Christians, magazine stories. Read fiction and poetry.

Few items on your "to do" list are more important than answering yes to the plea "Grandma, would you read me a story?"

Give your grandchildren complete Bible answers to their spiritual questions. If the concepts are too hard for them to understand, give them the general idea anyway. Plant truth in their minds. The day will come when it makes sense to them.

Dealing with Grandchildren Who Are Unresponsive to the Gospel

How about those grandchildren who seem hostile to any form of Christian witness? How should you treat them?

Exactly the same as all the others.

Your striving to share your faith is a statement about you. You're reinforcing to them that this is something real to you, something crucial in your life, something that for you is real, alive, and valid.

When Renée was seven years old, her grandmother gave her a Bible. It didn't happen to be a children's Bible with easy words or pleasant pictures. It was just an inexpensive King James Version. Renée looked at it a time or two and stuck it in the back of a dresser drawer. After that, her grandmother often gave her Christian books for presents. But Renée threw those away. She didn't want any of her friends thinking she was "religious." She didn't toss the Bible, however, mainly out of superstition. It seemed like an unlucky thing to do.

At age 18 Renée married. As she packed her belongings, her sister reached into the dresser and tossed her the Bible.

"Here—this must be yours," she said. "It has your name on it."

Renée placed the Bible into a cardboard file box that contained high school annuals and other memorabilia from childhood. At her new home, that box was shelved out in the garage.

Since Renée's Husband, Owen, was not a Christian, they found no need to have a Bible in the house. It remained in that box through 7 moves and 2 childbirths.

One day, in a period of depression about the complexities of life and the helplessness she felt in trying to raise children, the thought occurred to Renée that some people found help in the Bible. Certainly her grandmother had.

Almost embarrassed to mention it to her husband, she finally said, "Owen, why don't we start reading the Bible?"

To her surprise he said, "Sure." Then he added, "Do we have one?"

They rummaged through the garage and found the dusty black book with the cracking simulated leather cover. Night after night they read to each other after the children were in bed. The more they read, the more they realized their separation from God.

After several months, they began to attend a church in town. A few weeks later at a home Bible study, they learned how to become a Christian. Later that month both Renée and Owen accepted Jesus as Lord of their lives.

Twenty years later, they now serve in full-time Christian ministry.

It took 17 years for the present from Grandma to be read. But the conversion of Renée and her husband was no accident.

We cannot force our children or our grandchildren to become Christians. But we can make sure every one of them has an opportunity to hear the gospel.

It's our duty and our supreme privilege.

10

The Power of Loving Discipline

Just about the time a woman thinks her work is done,
she becomes a grandmother.
—Edward H. Dreschnack

Saturdays are lousy days to go to an amusement park, but sometimes Saturday is all you have. So there we stood in line with Aaron waiting for 35 minutes for some gadget to whirl us unmercifully through space until we all had stomach cramps. As we did, we watched one lady with youngster in tow.

"Gwendolyn, you are going to sit!" she barked as she flopped down on a bench and sighed deeply.

"Grandma, we haven't finished." The little girl pranced from one foot to another.

"Sit down!" The grandmother spoke with such a forceful tone that most of the small children standing in line around us started to sit.

"Oh, Grandma—this isn't any fun," Gwendolyn pouted.

"Fun?" Grandma wailed, "You spilled Coke all over my dress on the train ride. You got scared at the top of Mystery Mountain, and we had to walk back down. You ordered the most expensive dinner in the restaurant and then wouldn't eat it. You cried for a glass dinosaur and then broke it. You've had me standing in lines for almost six hours. How much more fun do you think Grandma can take? Young lady, sit down!"

Gwendolyn sat down for about 30 seconds, then jumped up and ran to stand in line for something called the Suicide Chute. Grandma struggled from the bench and disappeared into the crowd.

We're sure they'll both look back on this as a memorable day. But we're not sure they'll think of it as a good memory.

How do you get your grandchildren to mind?

Getting Grandchildren to Mind

Accept the fact that you do not have the prime responsibility to train them in proper behavior.

Unless they're under your total care, your role is secondary in helping them acquire manners and discipline.

Fourteen-year-old Kitty struggles with her classes in school. Her eating habits aren't too good, contributing to a poor complexion. In addition, both you and her mother disapprove of her wardrobe.

On Friday night Kitty bounces into your house, pecks you on the cheek, grabs a Mountain Dew out of the refrigerator, and heads for your den and the telephone. You haven't seen her in a few weeks and look forward to a chance to talk.

So what are your goals for the weekend?

Easy. You'll give her a lecture on why she needs to study more, you'll pump six healthy meals into her body, you'll buy her some decent clothes, and you'll ban the phone.

Hold it. It can't be done. No kid on earth can change that much, that fast.

Focus on one doable goal and leave the rest alone for now. Just for the weekend, aim to move her beyond TV and telephones. Get tickets for a musical play, or take her bowling. Promise her pizza, and let her wear anything that's moral. When you get home, let her call a friend. You can't change everything at once, but you can introduce her to one artistic or faith experience in a weekend.

Always expect the best from them. Let your grandchildren know that Grandma and Grandpa count on their best behavior. Be realistic, but view them from their highest potential.

Xavier is only six, and he never sits still. You've just bought him a new yellow shirt, and he wants to wear it to the Chinese restaurant for dinner. Your first thought is "No way! He'll squirm around and splatter food on it."

That's expecting the worst. It might be better to say, "Sure, Xavier. That shirt looks great on you. But you'll need to sit still during dinner so nothing gets spilled on it. I'm sure you can do that, right?"

Some behavior problems are serious because no one ever expected anything better of the child. Anticipating the best means we—

- are quick to forgive and allow the child to try again
- help them see beyond their present self-image
- give them a higher standard for which to aim

But they have to know what you expect.

Don't be shocked if Cody doesn't jump to his feet when a woman enters the room if he's never been taught to do so. Don't grind your teeth because your granddaughter won't sit still during an hour-long church service if she can't sit still in one place for 10 minutes at home.

Gently nudge the child toward acceptable behavior that fits the circumstance. Also remember to

- present only one lesson at a time.
- teach in privacy. (For instance, explain good manners when you're at home. Don't humiliate him or her at your neighbor's formal party.)
- teach behavior patterns that will help the child, not merely be convenient for you. Keep his or her best interest in mind.

Don't force them to act older than they are. An 8-year-old is not expected to act like a 20-year-old. The trouble is, we forget what age-appropriate behavior is.

Children under 10 choose a place to eat because of the free toy or the playground equipment. It has nothing to do with food.

Boys 12 to 18 choose a place to eat that offers the most food possible. Volume is the main ingredient—quality matters little.

Girls between 12 and 15 will enjoy a restaurant that offers views of and conversations with the cutest boys.

Girls between 16 and 18 will want very little food and will probably select a place where no one will notice them eating with their grandparents.

They're just acting their age.

Five-year-olds will love to go fishing with Grandpa and will cry to get to go. But after about six minutes they'll want to come home. Twelve-year-olds will fish with you all day long and half the night without tiring. Sixteen-year-olds know all there is to know about fishing and would rather you didn't tag along. Twenty-year-olds will really enjoy fishing again.

Nine-year-old boys shout, 12-year-old girls giggle, and 6-year-olds sing and dance on top of the kitchen table to get a little attention.

Encourage them to be considerate and show good manners. But don't punish them because they don't act like grown-ups. If the Lord wanted everyone to act mature, He would have skipped childhood and we'd all be born as adults.

Walk your talk. Live the example, model the behavior, and strive to exhibit what you want them to achieve. Paul boldly challenged, "Be imitators of me, just as I also am of Christ" (1 Cor. 11:1).

Remain calm. Refuse to raise your voice. Practice consistent kindness. Exhibit your best behavior. Then when they copy you, you won't risk humiliation.

Three key danger areas for us all are the following:

- *Prejudice*—a negative prejudgment of another person based solely on such external factors as a difference in race, social status, financial condition, or outward appearance (clothes, hair, skin color, and so on).
- *Gossip*—telling stories (true or untrue) about other people for their denigration and your personal profit.
- *Self-centeredness*—trying to arrange life events for your personal peace and comfort, no matter what it causes in others' lives.

Kids have it rough. For the first three years of their lives everyone wants them to walk and talk. Every visit to Grandma's house centers on how many steps are taken and how many times they say "Nana" or some equivalent. Then, just when they're getting good at running around and yakking, everybody tells them to sit down and be quiet.

In the midst of this confusion, grandparents have the freedom to focus on short-range and long-range goals.

Short-range goals include details like
- talking her out of wearing that bright red lipstick
- lecturing him about that D in English
- scolding him for saying "Yuck!" when his aunt kisses him
- insisting he eat lima beans before he gets any pie
- forbidding her to climb trees while wearing her Sunday dress
- requesting he eat the crust of his peanut-butter-and-jelly sandwich
- preventing her from tossing the rubber duck into the toilet
- forbidding him high decibels of music

We don't have to ignore these things. Rather, make sure our grandchildren know that these things aren't nearly as important to us as long-range aims such as
- knowing Jesus Christ as personal Lord and Savior
- unselfish love for other people
- a lifetime occupation that brings satisfaction and service
- marrying a Christ-centered mate who will bring out their best
- a responsible role in their community
- a stable home environment in which to raise your great-grandchildren
- making their gifts, talents, and ministries available to Christ's Body, the Church

The comparison of the two lists reminds us of the contrast between the urgent, pressing moment's crisis and our ultimate life goals.

Priorities simplify discipline.

When your grandchildren grasp how deeply you're committed to them, they'll try to please you in ordinary matters. This will allow you to let up on peripheral concerns, and that will result in fewer conflicts.

Explain "how come." Mom and Dad throw out a quick "Because I say so—that's why." But Grandpa and Grandma should take the time for explanations.

"Grandpa, why do we say a prayer before we eat?"

"Because it's a constant reminder that the Lord provides for all our daily needs."

"Grandma, why can't I rent this video?"

"Because some movies can mess up your mind. They put things into your head that can never be taken out."

"Grandpa, why do I need to shake hands with your friends?"

"Well, son, it's a friendly way to tell a person that you're happy to get to know them.

"Grandma, why do I have to drink milk?"

"Because it's filled with calcium. You've got growing bones that are made up of lots of calcium. Grandmas need calcium too."

Even if you aren't sure they understand the explanation or they don't accept your logic, they'll at least know that it isn't an arbitrary decision but is based on reason.

Whenever possible, explain the biblical basis for your behavior. Let them see you're striving to be obedient to the Bible. But remember these guidelines:

- Demonstrate your own obedience before you require it of them.

    When the chairman of the Women's Auxiliary canceled her talk for the second monthly meeting in a row, Sterling's grandmother announced, "Well, I'm certainly not going to the meeting tomorrow."

    Later, Sterling ran to her with a complaint. "Bobby won't share his cars. I'm not going to his dumb birthday party."

"Oh, no, Sterling," she scolded. "The Bible says we should forgive each other just as the Lord forgave us."

"At that moment," Sterling's Grandma confessed, "the Lord pricked my heart."

- Don't strain interpretations just to get them to behave.

Melissa asks, "Grandpa, why did Mr. Neillor die?"

Grandpa answers, "Oh, he drank too much whiskey, and you know what the Bible says: 'The wages of sin is death' [Rom. 6:23]."

That's a great verse, but is it an appropriate interpretation? Melissa may think that if she or anyone she loves ever sins, it will result in immediate death. That's not a biblical view.

- Don't say, "God will be mad at you if you misbehave," or "God will get you if you disobey."

That tactic might work—for a while. But chances are that when the child acts up again, there will not be lightning from heaven nor will the earth open up and swallow the little rascal. Sooner or later, the child figures that God doesn't care what he or she does or that you don't know what you are talking about—or both. Don't portray God as the mean judge in the sky. Far too many people have wrong views of what He's like, and we don't want to add to that number.

- Allow them to point out a weakness in your behavior.

Grandpa gave young Nathan a stern lecture on how the body is the temple of God, quoting 1 Cor. 6:19-20 as a proof text: "Do you not know that your body is a temple of the Holy Spirit who is in you, whom you have from God, and that you are not your own? For you have been bought with a price: therefore glorify God in your body."

Having completed his discourse on the evils of taking drugs that change the chemical makeup of the body, he then pulled out his favorite pipe, stuffed it full of tobacco, took a big, deep drag, and toddled off to the den to read.

Nathan may quote the same verse back to him, and a sensitive grandpa would listen.

• Express joy in obeying God's Word.

Tom Sawyer was right. If you make something seem fun, others are going to want to do it also. But you have an advantage over Tom. Obeying God's Word brings a lot more pleasure than painting a fence.

Jesus says, "My yoke is easy and My burden is light" (Matt. 11:30). God's Word isn't a burden we drag around in agony. It's a lifestyle that adds to the quality of life.

If you're known as Kevin's grumpy, complaining, Christian grandmother, there's no motivation.

It's true, of course, that Christians confront plenty of tough, rough stuff. But we can still be filled with "love, joy, peace, patience, kindness, goodness, faithfulness, gentleness, self-control" (Gal. 5:22-23).

Let them see you as someone who is still growing and still trying to become the person God wants you to be. It's not that kids view their grandparents as always perfect. What they see most often are older people who refuse to change.

We're going to blow it sometimes in front of the grandkids. We don't have to be perfect, but we have to be willing to admit our mistakes and want to change. Listen to these assessments:

"Grandpa always complains about the preacher's sermon."

"Mama says Grandma's had that habit most all her life. There's no way she can stop it now."

Some say it's the privilege of growing older. You're settled in. Life's orderly, predictable. You're leary of surprises. So you lock in your actions, your emotions, your attitudes. You hunker down in a bunker mentality: "This is who I am. Love me or leave me." You fight anyone who tries to budge you from your well-earned position.

But that's not the faith life. Paul never settled for complacency. He wrote, "One thing I do: forgetting what lies behind and reaching forward to what lies ahead, I press on toward the goal for the prize of the upward call of God in Christ Jesus"

(Phil. 3:13-14).

The world is not divided into a power system in which the older rule the younger and the only chance to change sides is to live long enough. We're all in the same place, no matter what the age, striving to please God and be obedient to Him. Discipline of grandchildren will be more authentic if they see us as fellow learners.

Little Ben is having a terrible time playing with your neighbor's son. Ben keeps grabbing Dylan's toys and bringing them into your house.

"But I can't help it, Grandpa. I really like that red truck."

"But we must respect other people's things," Grandpa opines. He follows up with a personal story. "There's a gray beach house up on Cypress Point. I've wanted that place for years. I've prayed that the owners would give it up and that I could have it then. Now I realize I'll never have that house. It was hard to give it up. But God's in control of things like that. I'm learning to be content with what I have."

A bumper sticker reads, "Grandkids are so much fun, we should have had them first."

Delightful grandchildren are a joy, but disobedient grandchildren are less than a joy. You might not be able to change the disobedient into the delightful in one weekend, but you can make progress.

Shelly sat at the table in her grandmother's kitchen. Her eyes brightened as we entered the room. She seemed pleased that the speakers at church were going to have dinner with her grandmother, grandfather, and her.

She propped her hands under her chin. "My name's Shelly, and I'll be nine years old on December 25. Don't you dare say, 'Poor thing!' because I enjoy having my birthday on Christmas."

Caught off guard, we stared in surprise.

"Well," she announced, "don't mind me. I'm impossible to live with, you know."

"You are?" we said.

"Why, yes. My mother tells me that all the time. If I were

you, I wouldn't eat any of the peas. Grandma burnt them and then tried to hide it by melting garlic butter on top. Didn't you, Grandma?"

The entire meal was dominated by one precocious little girl.

"We keep her quite often," the grandmother later confessed. "Her mom and dad are going through a divorce, and neither seems in too much of a hurry to have Shelly."

For almost nine years she has had little concern shown her unless she forced her way into the situation. Now, for a short visit every month or so, Grandma and Grandpa will try to teach loving discipline.

A year later we saw Shelly again.

"Are you still quite impossible to live with?" we asked with a laugh.

"Of course," she snapped back. "But I suppose Grandma has domesticated me to some small degree."

We shook our heads in amazement.

Later, when Shelly was outside riding a horse, her grandparents explained.

"We've had Shelly a lot this year. And she's still a handful. But she's made several close friends at school, for the first time in her life."

"And," Grandma continued, "she hasn't griped about my cooking for over three months. That's definitely an improvement!"

Some might conclude that's not much progress. But it's not bad for grandparents who see a grandchild only on occasion. It's possible to influence them and still keep them loving you in the process.

That's what the legacy of good grandparenting is all about.

11

The Power of Top-Quality Time Together

If becoming a grandmother was only a matter of choice, I should advise every one of you straight way to become one. There is no fun for old people like it!
—Hannah Whitall Smith

"What is your favorite memory of your grandparents?"

We asked that question to dozens of grandchildren. We expected a multitude of different answers. In fact, we were counting on a long list that would give us a source of ideas to share with you in this book.

What we found out is that almost every response to that question began with these words: "I remember one vacation when I was at my grandparents' house. . . ."

Every time.

The kids are going to remember your house most of all.

"I loved vacations at Grandma's. I always had a great big bed and a room all to myself."

"Vacations were the best. Grandpa would take me down to the playground every day."

"You know what my granny would do? She would fix biscuits and gravy for breakfast any day I asked. I guess in the olden days people really liked to cook."

"When I went to their house, I would ride the electric bus downtown with Grandpa. Those buildings were as tall as mountains. We went into this big store, and there was a man with a uniform who held it open for us. I remember he said,

'Good morning, Mr. Temple.' I was impressed that he knew my grandfather's name. That was my first trip to a big city."

"My granddad ran this little grocery store on the border of Kansas and Oklahoma. I'd spend a week or two out there each summer. He'd sit me up on a box behind the counter and let me operate the cash register. There was no greater thrill during those first 12 years of my life. I thought those days would never end."

"Grandma always let me do fancy things when I went to her house. She'd get out her best silver tea service, and then we'd bake a plate of fancy little cookies. Then we'd dress up in our best clothes, just the two of us for tea. I bet it looked kind of silly, but I'll never forget those days as long as I live."

"My grandpa was a quiet, hardworking man. He didn't relax and joke very often. He always seemed so serious. But I loved going to the farm. The summer I was 13 I stayed for a whole month, and he taught me how to train horses. I think he enjoyed it as much as I did. When it was time to go, he hugged me, and I saw tears rolling down his cheeks. It was the only time I ever saw him cry."

The stories just go on and on. There's a love relationship between grandkids and vacations at Grandma and Grandpa's.

How to Make Their Stay a Real Vacation

Set Aside Time to Do It Right

If you're not yet retired, you'll want to make arrangements for your vacation time to blend with your grandchildren's visits. This will probably mean some advance planning.

Grandpa might say, "Well, Grandma's at home with the grandkids. I'll go ahead and work."

Sure, if there's absolutely no other alternative. But taking away time from the grandkids is not a whole lot different from stealing money from their piggy bank. You're taking something precious from them that can never be replaced.

If you see your grandchildren quite often, then perhaps you should keep with your regular schedule. If you see them very seldom, then take your vacation time with them.

Many grandparents are retired or have flexible schedules. Did you ever wonder what your eulogy will sound like? What will the family say when they stand around your casket? A lot of memories are going to start out, "Do you remember that time we spent a week at Grandma and Grandpa's?" Those are the memories you're creating now. For the most part, you'll be remembered for those few short days together.

How much time do you need to do it right? Some folks recommend one day for each year of age. Have the 3-year-old stay for 3 days, the 6-year-old for 6 days, the 10-year-old for 10 days, and so on. But all of that varies depending on time, distance, health, money, and the ability to take them one at a time.

Aim for a week. That will give you time to do a variety of weekday and weekend activities, including worshiping together.

If their parents can't afford to send the kids to your house, do whatever you can to help with the costs. Perhaps you had the idea to leave each of the grandkids a couple thousand dollars' inheritance. It would be better to invest in airline tickets while you're still around. The impact will be far greater and more lasting.

Focus Your Entire Time on Your Grandchild

There might be an occasional circumstance when it's impossible to focus all your time on your grandchild, but set it as your goal. Cancel your weekly bowling league, reschedule the art class, and replace the shock absorbers on the car some other time. You can paint the garage some other week and host the women's Bible study next month. Give this time to your grandchildren.

This makes a statement to your grandchildren and others about what's important to you. It also might be the only time in the child's life when he or she commands the undivided attention of an adult. Mom visits while she cooks dinner and drives to band practice. Dad talks over the top of the newspaper or during television commercials.

Sure, Dad plays catch, but he has only a few minutes after dinner and before he has to run to another meeting. Mom wants to look at all the doll clothes but has to hurry to get ready for work every morning.

One small boy wrote, "I don't think my grandma and grandpa have very many friends. When I go to visit them, they don't have anyone to talk to but me. They never seem to have anywhere to go. They just want to play. It must be fun to be a grandparent. I think I'll be a grandfather when I am very, very old."

Arrange the Timing of Their Visit

You'll need to consider the following:

The season of the year. If you live in Florida, the summer might be too hot and sweltering for a boy from Colorado. If you live in Minnesota, perhaps January is too cold for your Arizona granddaughter. On the other hand, the extreme change might be an added attraction.

The age of the child. The 12-year-old will love swimming in the lake, but that happens only in the summer. The 5-year-old is afraid of water, so it doesn't matter whether he or she comes during the swimming season or some other time of the year. Your 16-year-old will have cheerleading practice in August, so you'd better schedule something in early summer for her.

The interests of the child. John likes to water ski, so ask him to come in July. Tina loves to downhill ski; invite her during Christmas break. Rhet likes to fish; ask him to come in early June, when the water is high and the trout are big. Little Sarah loves animals, so you can take her to the zoo when it's open. And Geoffry? If there are cookies, he'll come any day of the year.

The activities in your area. If your grandson is an avid baseball fan, invite him to your place in Phoenix in March for spring training. If you have a big boat show coming up in August, ask your granddaughter who loves boat races. When the Shakespeare festival hits town, invite the budding actor or actress to come visit.

Any week would be good for a visit, but some weeks will be better than others.

Invite Your Grandkids to Come Visit One at a Time

Granted, it might be impossible to have your grandchildren to come visit one at a time, but you can give it a try.

The more grandkids you have, the more they need time by themselves. If you have to bunch them up, then how about a couple of compatible cousins instead of siblings?

Why have them one at a time?

- It might be the only time they get a break from their family and their family gets a break from them.
- It gives them a chance to seek their individual identity apart from the others.
- It will help you get to know each as a person instead of as part of a group.
- Because most kids act better alone without the family pecking order. There's no little brother to fight with and no big sister pestering.
- You can concentrate on this one's likes and dislikes. Jannie loves Chinese food. Justin hates it. Justin loves Italian food. Jannie hates it. When you have them both over, where do you eat out? At the taco restaurant. But when you have them one at a time, each is delighted to get to choose the restaurant.
- For many, it's their first attempt to survive apart from their parents. You'll be there to help them. They may not want a brother or sister witnessing this struggle.

The most precious memories we hear about from grandkids involve "just me and my grandma" or "just me and Grandpa."

"It's no exaggeration," Marty relates. "When we were kids, the most exciting time of the year was our individual trips to Grandma and Grandpa's house. I think we felt as though we had each won a sweepstakes. I can still remember the feeling of seeing my sisters stare out the back window of our family car as they drove away, leaving me behind at Grandma and Grandpa's. They always looked like puppies going to the pound. I felt so proud, I wanted to salute."

Know the Activities in Your Area for Kids Their Age

Ask some of the kids at church what the fun things to do in town are. Ask them—

- "Where is your favorite place to eat out?"
- "Where's the best store to shop?"
- "If you had an afternoon to do anything in this area you wanted, what would it be?"
- "Which park has the best play equipment?"

Call the local chamber of commerce or visitors' center to find out upcoming activities. A car show at the mall. A concert at the civic auditorium. A circus at the fairgrounds. Or how about a bike ride along the levy?

When your 10-year-old bursts through the door with "What's happenin', Grandma?" you'll know how to answer that question better than anyone else in town.

Don't Forget the Historical Points of Interest

Your local historical sites might be so common to you that you forget they're there. Again, the chamber of commerce, the visitors' center, or your local historical society might have some maps that show the highlights.

We love living in northern Idaho. You might not think too much happens here. You've probably never heard of towns like Winchester, Weippe, Grangeville, and Dixie.

Just down the hill a few miles from our house is the Clearwater River. Lewis and Clark floated down that very spot in 1805. Not far southeast of our house the Nez Percé Indian War began in 1877. It is considered one of the most masterful military retreats in history. Only 25 miles from our front door is the lower entrance to Hell's Canyon, the deepest gorge in the United States. Up on the other side of the Clearwater stands the ruins of the first gold mine discovered in this state. Not too far from it you can find prospectors still digging for gold. We live just south of the Palouse region, where Appaloosa horses, famous for the spots on their rumps, originated.

There are interesting points of history and geography in every region.

So scout around. For each one, find out
- how to get there
- the best time of the day to visit
- the costs involved
- how much time it takes to view the site
- how long it will take to drive there and back
- if there are any places to eat along the way

Teach your grandchildren local history.

Some of your grandkids will not seem to be the least interested. However, you don't have to ask them if they want to go—just take them. Kids seldom have an accurate view of the importance of things. But the day will come when it all comes back to them and they say, "Hey—I went there with my grandparents once."

"That sounds like a very intense and tiring week."

Sure. Why else have we been eating oat bran and wheat germ all year? Just why is it we want to live long, be strong and healthy? To enjoy the family.

All right, get ready—here come the grandkids!

Traveling with Grandchildren

What about grandparents who are still working? We're certainly among them. Or the ones who just don't have facilities for grandkids in their home? Or the grandparents who love to travel and are almost always on the road? The solution? Take the grandkids on vacation with you.

Many of the home rules given in earlier chapters still apply.

1. Remember the days-years formula given earlier in the chapter. Four-year-olds travel for four days, eight-year-olds for eight, and so on.

2. Make sure your travel vehicle fits the child. Don't cram four grandkids in the back seat of a compact car for a 500-mile trip.

3. Take them one at a time if possible. How about as a present on each of their 12th birthdays? or 10th? or 8th?

4. Know your highways. Will they be mountainous roads? Interstates? Unpaved roads? (Yes, there are still plenty of them left.)

5. Know the history of the region. Read up ahead of time and give your grandkids a running commentary of what happened where and when. Or bring along a place names book.

6. Grab a notebook. Record the animals, fauna, flowers, and geography you'll view. Jot down intriguing conversations. Describe the people you meet. Stop and show them the difference between pine, fir, and cedar trees. Walk along the beach and collect shells; then identify each one.

7. Know the endurance levels of the kids. How many miles before a rest room stop? A fast-food break? A playground?

8. Have some ideas for conversations and games as you travel. A whole industry flourishes by producing car games for kids. Ask at your nearest toy store, or check at the bookstore. But the best games will be the ones you invent along the way.

9. Keep some exciting destinations just ahead. In the long miles in between, tell them about the cave you'll explore, the mountain you'll climb, or the waterfall you'll stand under at the next stop.

10. Let them make some of the decisions. Will it be McDonald's or Burger King? Will you stay the night at the Riverview or the Silver Palace? Will you visit the modern art museum or the miniature golf course?

11. Challenge them to new experiences. Help them climb to the top of a volcano, raft down the river, ride on the sternwheeler. Dine in the Mongolian restaurant. Hike across the Civil War battlefield. Sail on a boat across the harbor. Sample the entries in the chili cook-off. Watch the Indian tribal dance.

12. Give them a break from the grind of travel. Stay an extra day in one place so they (and you) can rest up. Stop at a city park every few hours. Let them run off some pent-up energy. Get to a motel early enough for them to swim or play catch so they can unwind.

13. Look for points of spiritual interest along the way. Show them the campgrounds where Billy Sunday once preached. Drive by the famous 10,000-member church. Visit

the campuses of Christian colleges, even when the grandkids are young, to give them some future goals

If they live in a city, take them to the country. If they live by the ocean, take them to the desert. If they live on the plains, take them to the mountains.

Check out national parks, adjoining states, neighboring foreign countries, state capitals, famous resort areas, and remote, secluded coves.

Most kids will like any place as long as Grandma and Grandpa are there.

Ask yourself, "Where did I want to go when I was that age?" Did you ever make it? Did they? If not, why not make this the year you finally go?

As you travel, it's a good time to read verses together, to pray for the Lord's safety and leading. Take time in the evening to thank God for the events of the day. Point out God's handiwork wherever you go. Find a good church, and attend Sunday School and worship together. Help them to perceive that God is with you wherever you go.

What will the grandkids gain?

- A closeness to their grandparents. Shared new experiences sink deep in the memory.
- Creativity. Traveling stimulates the mind.
- More possibilities for the future by seeing a bigger, wider world.
- Opportunity to miss their families and their normal routines.

What will the children's parents gain?

- About three more hours of sleep every night.
- A chance to work on relationships with the other children or each other.
- An example for them to copy in future years.
- A time to really miss the kids.

And what will you gain?

- New respect for what it is like to be a kid in today's world.
- The joy of seeing the world through a kid's eyes again.

- An understanding for the challenge their parents face.
- About 200 hugs and a couple dozen smooches.

Steve spent most of his childhood years living across the street from one set of grandparents and two doors away from the other.

"Hardly a day would go by that I wasn't in one house or the other, or both. I played games, sang songs, ate lots of meals, and visited with both sides constantly.

"But they've been gone for years now. My memory of them is beginning to fade. If you asked me to tell you all about them, well, I'd have some trouble, especially on the Bly side. Grandma and Grandpa were people of the land. Their hard-earned farm took most of their attention. They seldom got away from it. But I do remember my grandmother a little better than my grandfather. You see, two different times Grandmother took me on a vacation with her. I remember both of those trips well.

"On the other side of the family I have plenty of fond memories still. Every summer I traveled to the coast with my Grandma and Grandpa Wilson. I remember featherbeds and fireworks, tom cods and halibuts, boardwalks and the penny arcades. We would stop at Tiny's for breakfast and a place that served artichoke milk shakes for lunch. And sometimes we cruised along the Seventeen Mile Drive to see how the rich folks lived.

"I remember it all, from Grandpa's deep laugh to Grandma's warm hug.

"I was just a kid then—a kid on vacation, a kid on vacation with Grandma and Grandpa."

There are some things that are priceless.

12

The Power of Being the World's Best Baby-Sitter

A grandmother is the only baby-sitter
who doesn't charge more after midnight—
or anything before midnight.
—Erma Bombeck

The tanned couple sat down next to us for dinner at a conference in Arizona. The conversation turned from the weather to children to grandchildren. The question popped up, "Are grandparents good baby-sitters?"

"We can't help you there," the man replied. "We only have one child. She and her family live in Montana, so we don't really get a chance to baby-sit."

"Oh, that's too bad," we consoled. "How about when you raised your own daughter? Did you find that your parents made good baby-sitters?"

"They never baby-sat. We weren't going to leave our little Julia with anyone else. We never had any baby-sitter, ever. If we couldn't take her along, we just didn't go."

"Never?" we gasped.

"Nope."

Then his wife added, "Well, there was just one time that my mother watched her for an hour or so."

Then he boomed back, "But that was it. No sir, we weren't going to let someone else raise our kid."

Their "kid" is now 47 years old. How we wanted to hear the story from her point of view!

But that family is an extreme—we hope.

Bud and Cleo rejoiced when Danny, Margie, and the boys moved back to town. It was going to be great to have the children and grandchildren living right on the same block. No more driving six hours across the desert to get to their house.

The grandkids spent most of the summer in Bud and Cleo's swimming pool, which gave their folks some time to get unpacked and move in. When school started in the fall, the schedule changed—a little.

Margie decided to finish college, so this meant going to school Tuesdays and Thursdays. Cleo thought she could surely watch the kids a couple days a week, even though Bud was still working long hours.

She hadn't counted on Margie's night school class and Danny's bowling league on Tuesday nights. Sometimes the boys just spent the night at Grandma and Grandpa's. When the second semester rolled around, the school schedule was shifted to Monday, Wednesday, and Friday. And this year, Margie decided to take classes five days a week until she graduated. Now she hints about going to graduate school.

Bud and Cleo dearly love their kids and their grandkids, but they're worn out. They hate to admit that, so they struggle along, playing the martyr, straining their last nerve.

Their situation is an extreme—we hope.

Most of the rest of us fit somewhere in between.

In surveying parents across the country, we find a nearly unanimous consensus that leaving the kids with the grandparents is the next best thing to being with them yourself. And in some cases, it's even better.

Why Parents Like Grandparent Baby-Sitters

There are several reasons that parents like using their own parents as baby-sitters. Here are just a few:

They have years of experience. Thirteen-year-old girls can make terrific baby-sitters, but you worry a bit. What if Kevin throws up all over the sofa? What if Kiley cuts her finger?

What if some irate stranger appears at the front door? What if little Jessica tries that "I'm going to hold my breath until I get my way" trick? Grandparents have been through it all. "If they can raise a kid like me," the parents reason, "then they can handle anything."

They have a preestablished relationship with the children. Tammy's best friend at church recommends a woman who's new in town and really loves children. She's mature, experienced, caring. But she doesn't know little Nicole, who is extremely shy at meeting new people. She can go a whole evening without speaking a word. A baby-sitter has to be really sensitive with her.

So Tammy turns to Nicole's grandparents. Nicole dearly loves to go to Grandpa and Grandma's. They know how to draw her out of her shell. She'll go with them places even her parents can't get her to go.

They have ownership in the children. Other folks, no matter how caring, don't have blood ties to these children. For some, baby-sitting is just a job. There's no reason to get too personal. For others, they sincerely pay attention to the children—but only during the time they're together.

Grandparents are different. They care about the kids all the time. Their world seems to rotate around these little ones. They know what Jonathan likes to eat, what he wants for his birthday, and why he had a rotten day at school.

Grandparents care about who they are, how they feel, what they want to be when they grow up, who they will someday marry, how they feel about themselves, and whether their socks match.

They provide a familiar environment for the children. Grandparents can come to the kids' house and know the routine. You don't have to tell them where you keep the emergency ration of cookies, where the dryer is in case Peter doesn't have clean jammies, or where to find bandages for Haley's skinned-up knee. Besides, Grandmas are noted for washing the dishes, cycling a couple of loads of clothes, and vacuuming the living room before Mom and Dad back out of the driveway. Grandpas seem to delight in replacing light bulbs, fixing screen doors, watering the dry lawn, and inventing a little gadget that keeps the dishwasher from plugging up so often.

If the kids are brought to Grandma and Grandpa's house, there's a bigger advantage for parents, like not having to clean the house. It's a familiar place for the kids. They already know where the toys are stored, what rooms are off limits, and where Grandma's candy jar is.

Grandparents need little supervision from the parents. A grandparent doesn't need to be called halfway through the evening to see if all is well, and the parents rarely receive a desperation call either. There's no need to give them the phone number of the nearest hospital, a neighbor, a lawyer, and above all else, a plumber. They'll survive on their own.

No list is needed of what Crissy won't eat or what Mason needs to wear to bed. It's the one place the kids can be let off at the curb with Grandpa standing in the doorway and not have another worry.

Grandparents are inexpensive. To be honest, this is a great delight to parents. The amount saved for baby-sitting can pay for dinner.

A few years back we ran a program at our church offering free baby-sitting one Friday night per month. We wanted to strengthen husband-wife relationships and felt every couple deserved one night a month to themselves. It was a huge success.

Several wives told us that it was the first time since the children were born that they had been out on a date alone with their hubbies. "It's too hard to get good sitters," one said, "and Barry says we really can't afford it." Without fail, those who took advantage of the program most were families whose grandparents lived far away.

Kids Enjoy Grandparent Baby-Sitters

Kids are free to be themselves. In a new relationship there's a lot of awkward time just trying to find out what the baby-sitter is like and what they expect and how one should act. With Grandma, the child's not afraid to giggle or cheer at the ball game on television or run around in his or her underwear.

"It's just Grandma and Grandpa. They like me the way I am."

Kids feel loved. Even animals can sense when they're truly loved. How much more can children! "Grandma might not feel good, and Grandpa might be tired, but they still love me."

They get undivided attention. "I went to my grandma's last night," one little girl told us, "and we were playing a game when the phone rang. Grandma answered it and said, 'I'm sorry—I'm busy playing a game with my granddaughter. Could you call back tomorrow?' Grandma really likes to play games with me."

Kids feel secure with Grandpa and Grandma. "We had a big lightning storm last night, but my grandpa lit some candles. We sat on the couch next to him, and he told stories about when he was camping out in the woods one summer and never had any electricity. He let us stay right there until the lights came on again. My grandpa isn't afraid of anything."

Kids enjoy getting spoiled. "We had cookies and ice cream right before dinner," Brenton brags. "And Grandpa took us down to the mall for a walk and bought us a toy. And they let me stay up until nine. Grandma always fixes too much food, so I'm supposed to eat a lot. Grandpa let me play with his computer. Boy, if I couldn't live at home, I would sure want to live with my grandma and grandpa."

Grandparents have this habit of buying things, making things, giving away things. Grandkids love it. The only problem the kids have is leaving.

But as a growing number of grandparents have realized, when it becomes necessary for the grandkids to come live with them full-time, the relationship alters. When grandparents switch to parenting, the rules shift. What works for a temporary stay doesn't apply for permanent residency.

Why Grandparents Sometimes Hate to Baby-sit

If parents love it and the kids love it, why is it that grandparents sometimes hate to baby-sit?

Let's face it. Caring for grandchildren is not always ice cream and gumdrops. Sometimes it's pure grit and groan. What causes the problems?

Perhaps it's because of physical limitations. There's a good reason why the prime childbearing years are 18 to 28. No matter how great a shape you try to maintain, 60 is not 30. And 70 is nowhere near 40. On top of that, if you develop weak knees, a bad back, stiff joints, or any of those other lovely signs of aging, certain aspects of grandparenting spell physical agony.

This produces a mental strain, too, because you would like to have the stamina to enjoy the grandkids more. Though you look forward to their company, you may sigh with relief when they leave.

Perhaps it's because parents have not taught their kids any discipline or respect. Some grandkids are simply difficult to handle. They refuse to mind you, reject your correction, destroy your belongings, bother the neighbors, embarrass your friends, and act as if you owed them the stars when you would like to send them to the moon. You can blame them, or you can blame their parents. Either way, you groan when you see them coming, especially if the parents refuse to allow you to rein them in and you can't find the leverage for control. The best you can do is brace yourself for the human hurricane and hope it passes quickly—or decline to be alone with the kids.

Perhaps it's because grandparents are not always told the parents' rules of the game. Mothers have been known to assume that grandparents understand more than they do. You feed Ethan chocolate cake, and your daughter has a fit. "He's allergic to chocolate," she informs you.

You allow Jamie to watch a cartoon show, and your son berates you for your lack of judgment. "We don't want her watching that one. Too much violence."

You allow Jasmine to use her cell phone and then find out her parents never want her to call that guy again.

Nobody told you the rules until after you had broken them. It's easy to get gun shy.

Sometimes grandparents just aren't equipped to handle the particular situation. The parents bring two-year-old Trent but not the high chair. So you have to sit at the table holding a Jell-O-tossing, spinach-spitting, squirm bomb in your lap while you grab a bite to eat.

Madeleine is supposed to practice her cheerleading in your living room, but you live in a condo with a cranky couple in the unit under yours.

You're asked to help Ricky with his homework, but you don't have the foggiest notion how to do precalculus.

And what about the grandkids with special challenges—seizures, attention deficit disorder, and so on?

Lack of adequate advance notices makes grandparenting a strain. "Oh, Mom, glad we caught you at home. Jerry just called and wants me to meet him downtown. Hope you can keep the kids. Give Sam a bath, and Susan needs her hair washed, and take a look at Simon's hand—I don't think he'll need stitches. We'll try to get back by 12:30 or 1:00. If it's going to be later, we'll call. Have fun!"

Perhaps it's because of unresolved differences with the parents of the grandchildren. Your daughter-in-law thinks you're far too strict with the grandchildren, yet your son keeps bringing them over. You feel tense the whole evening, wondering what you should do and say to make everyone happy. The kids sense your discomfort and act up, which doubles your anxiety.

We have no idea if Jesus ever had the responsibility of baby-sitting His younger brothers and sisters. But He never seemed to mind the interruptions of children.

> They were bringing children to Him so that He might touch them; but the disciples rebuked them. But when Jesus saw this, He was indignant and said to them, "Permit the children to come to Me; do not hinder them; for the kingdom of God belongs to such as these. Truly I say to

you, whoever does not receive the kingdom of God like a child shall not enter it at all." And He took them in His arms and began blessing them, laying His hands upon them (Mark 10:13-16).

Perhaps the lines "Permit the children to come to Me" and "He took them in His arms and began blessing them" should be a grandparent's theme verses.

So how can we make that happen in the best possible way?

Develop a Basic Baby-Sitting Strategy

Kid-proof your house. No, don't sell your furniture and trade the china for Corelle, unless you really want to. Walk around your place and look for obvious trouble spots for curious eyes and hands. Check out rugs that slip, glass figurines perched on low coffee tables, fireplace matches on the hearth instead of the mantel, chairs too frail for a six-year-old's jumps, and cleaning supplies in low cupboards. Scout the yard for undefined flower beds that could be easily turned into end zones for football games or unfilled mud holes.

You don't want to spend the entire time yelling, "No! Don't touch that." Make changes that will smooth the relationship.

Purchase some necessary items. If the budget's tight, try the thrift store or discount department store.

Provide your own high chair, playpen, or crib. Consider a swing for the backyard. A basketball hoop is handy over the garage door. How about an extension phone in the den and a video player?

If you have a stereo, buy headphones. In fact, buy two sets. That way your grandchild can share his or her latest tape with a friend—or grandma.

Build a guardrail on the bed. Stretch an expandable gate across the stairs. Invest in colored plastic picnic dishes for their dinnerware. Own at least one stretch-your-feet-out-on-it couch and a bedspread that can be tossed into the washer when decorated with fudge handprints.

Pile up the pantry. A good supply of emergency nonperishables come in handy—some favorite soups, packages of hot chocolate mix and puddings, a few of those horrid little squiggly noodles and tasteless meatballs they love, and of course, the world's favorite—macaroni and cheese.

If you don't get a chance to purchase what you need before they arrive, load them into the car and hit the supermarket first thing. They'll be charmed to help you make choices.

Ask basic questions. Every time the grandkids are dropped off, check on their specific bedtimes. Tell Mom what you were planning to feed them, and get her approval. Find out the evening's "dos and don'ts." Ask about television programs, bedtime wear, and rules for using the telephone.

Volunteer before you're asked. If you always volunteer, then the children's parents will know for sure you want to baby-sit, and you can be specific about which times you're available. If, for example, you and your mate attend a home Bible study every Wednesday night, then volunteer for "any night except Wednesday." You can say, "We'd love to have them once a week," which also says that more often than that might be too much.

Learn to say no. It would be best if your kids asked you to care for the kids only at convenient times. But there are times when it's not. Practice saying no.

But explain your reasons. "Grandpa's sick." "I have to work tonight." "We have other plans."

Then offer to help them find a sitter: "I'll call someone from the church" or "I'll check with my neighbor's daughter."

If you can, volunteer for your next available time. "I'm sorry, honey, but we can't do it on Friday. We'd be happy to have the kids on Saturday, though."

Make sure they all know your rules. Both the parents and grandkids need to know the rules of your house. So tell them.

But you need some rules for yourself as well. Grandparents must abide by principles if they want good relationships and if they're serious about leaving a legacy. The following are a few suggestions.

Grandparent No-No's

- Never ignore the opinions or orders of the parents.
- Never bicker with your mate in front of the grandchildren.
- Never berate a grandchild in front of others.
- Never abandon a child in front of the television set. Make sure you control what is watched whether it's network, cable, movie videos, or games.
- Never knowingly fill the children with fear by recounting violent news accounts, telling scary stories, and so on.
- Be sensitive to the long-range health of the children when tempted to stuff them with treats.

Our Zachary was diagnosed with attention deficit hyperactivity disorder and was prescribed Ritalin. After several years our daughter-in-law Lois determined to try to treat Zachary with a strict diet regimen, especially eliminating foods with artificial coloring and sweetners, and wean him off the Ritalin. The next time he came to Grandma and Grandpa's, we were ready to cooperate. We purchased a special cookbook with recipes geared to his dietary requisites. We told Zachary he could eat "anything listed in this book." That way, we assisted Lois in her campaign, yet he had some interesting options different from home. So we baked a turkey and sweet potato casserole, even though it wasn't Thanksgiving.

Make your own list geared to your family situation.

"Who's your favorite baby-sitter?" we asked Willie.

"My grandma," he shot back.

"Why do you like her best?"

When Willie smiled, his toothless front gums showed. "Because I get things."

"What kind of things?"

"Oh, Matchbox cars, marbles, money for my piggy bank— things like that. Besides, I get to play with Buford."

"Who's Buford?"

"Buford is Grandma's stuffed buffalo. No one can touch him but me and her."

"So you like being there because you get things?"

"Yep. And because Grandma's real nice."

"How is she nice?"

"She likes me. She doesn't yell, and she won't bite."

"Do some people not like you?"

"Sure. But Grandma likes me even if I'm naughty."

"Are you naughty very often?"

"Nope. But even if I was, Grandma would still let me stay at her house." Willie stopped to scratch his cheek. "I had a dream about her last night."

"You did? What was it about?"

"It was real scary. I was lost, and I couldn't find my house. I mean, it wasn't on the right street, and there were some dogs chasing me and trying to eat me."

"Wow! What did you do?"

"I ran real hard to Grandma's house, and she let me in."

Grandparents know how to take really good care of kids.

13

The Power of Praying for Your Grandchildren

*Elijah was a man with a nature like ours,
and he prayed earnestly that it would not rain;
and it did not rain on the earth for three years and
six months. And he prayed again, and the sky
poured rain and the earth produced its fruit.*
—James 5:17-18

"We won't see our grandkids for five years."

Gary and Beverly are the parents of a missionary. Their grandchildren are genuine MKs (missionary kids). They'll grow up in a remote area of Paraguay. Jacob is now 10, Julie 7, and Justine 3. When they next see Grandma and Grandpa, they'll be 15, 12, and 8. They'll speak Spanish as fluently as English and feel culturally out of place in the United States.

So how can Gary and Beverly act as good grandparents? They can make sure that the kids have what they need more than anything else in the world: regular communication and prayer.

Your grandkids live clear across the country? Broken relationships and divorce make it impossible for you to even see them? Perhaps they're all grown and gone their separate ways, seldom making contact with you. What's your responsibility in such cases?

The primary function of grandparenting—whether your grandchildren live across the street or around the globe, whether you see them every day or once in every 10 years—remains the same: praying for them

Elijah prayed very specific prayers: *Lord, stop the rain,* and later, *Lord, let it pour.* Sometimes we have lots of faith: *Lord, please heal this cancer. We know You're doing it right now.* Other times we can barely utter, *Lord, help them and us survive this day.*

They need more than just an occasional *Bless the grandchildren, Lord.* Here are some ideas for establishing an effective prayer ministry for your grandchildren.

Grandparents Who Are Serious About Prayer

Make a Picture Prayer Journal for Each of Your Grandkids

A picture prayer journal should be a working document, not a keepsake album. Make something simple, portable, and replaceable.

With a stenographer's pad, the kind you find at the supermarket, use a separate page for each grandchild. Write the child's full name across the top. Unless you're blessed with 75 grandkids, leave a blank page or two between grandchildren. That way the notebook will last longer before it fills up.

In the upper left-hand corner use a glue stick, and paste in the latest picture of the grandchild. Those little wallet-size school pictures work well. It could look like this:

[NOTEBOOK PAGE 1]

Jerome Lee Atwood
July 14, 1988

(photo)

[NOTEBOOK PAGE 4]

Jessica Lynn Atwood
July 19, 1991

(photo)

Fill up the blank pages with notes and prayer requests. The steno-size book will slip nicely into the back of most Bibles or purses. You can carry it with you or use it as a reminder each time you read your Bible.

Our friend Peggy found she had about 10 minutes of quiet time in the sanctuary between the closing of Sunday School and the beginning of the morning service each week. She uses this as a time of prayer for her grandchildren.

What goes into the prayer journal?

● The ordinary needs of kids.

Write down requests about their health and safety; mental, physical, and spiritual growth; peer pressure; strength to resist temptations from sex, drug abuse, and the like.

● Specific requests.

Every time you get a letter or phone call from a grandchild or from their parents, be alert for particular needs of the kids — things like the following:

Terry is worried about making the football team.

Tony sprained his wrist.

Tyler is having trouble with a kid on the school bus.

Tess is going to sing a solo in the children's choir.

Ted thinks his ears are too big.

Tonya thinks she'll die if she doesn't get straight A's.

Tom will be going to camp.

Travis has to have two teeth pulled.

Troy just broke up with his girlfriend.

If you use a pencil, you can add corrections and updates.

How often do you pray through your entire journal? That depends on your schedule, the number of grandchildren you have, and how many requests you have listed. Once a day is not too often. Once a month, for each one separately, would be the minimum. If you happen to have seven or fewer grandchildren, assign each one to a particular day of the week. (Wednesdays pray for Brad, Thursdays for Mark, Fridays for Michael, and so on.)

Develop a Monthly Prayer Calendar

An inexpensive yearly, month-by-month calendar will do—the kind the drug stores give away for free every Christmas. Make it small enough to fit into your purse, pocket, or Bible.

At the first of each year, write in all the grandchildren's birthdays.

As you hear of special events or happenings in their lives, jot down the date on your calendar. These are not necessarily appointments for events you'll attend (those should go on your main calendar). On the days you mark on the prayer calendar, you have special prayer for that particular grandchild.

Your calendar will be filled with items like

April 4: Janet gets her braces off.

April 9: Jamie's piano recital.

April 16: Jackie's birthday.

April 21: Joe gets baptized.

April 24: Jake takes the college entrance exam.

You may not be informed of all the events in your grandchildren's lives, but you can be faithful in praying for some. Each day, you and your spouse can glance at the grandkids' prayer calendar.

Prayer is a necessary exercise and a resourceful weapon in the arsenal of any grandparent. You've probably memorized the verses, as we have, such as James 5:16—"The effective prayer of a righteous man can accomplish much." Or Matt. 18:19-20—"If two of you agree on earth about anything that they may ask, it shall be done for them by My Father who is in heaven. For where two or three have gathered together in My name, there I am in their midst."

Two in agreement.

It takes one grandma and one grandpa or one grandparent and one parent to meet the requirements of this scripture.

Develop a Few "How To" Prayer Guides

It won't take long to discover what topics are key for you as you pray for your grandchildren. The following seven needs can serve as starting points.

Pray for their education—
- that God will give them a desire to do their best
- that their minds will be challenged
- for their teachers
- for their school system
- that a balance of subjects and ideas will be presented
- for a safe, healthful classroom environment
- for courage to speak biblical truth even in the classroom
- for learning God's lessons for them
  - *to learn facts and principles that prepare them for a future career*
- that they will learn lessons much deeper than report cards and achievement tests can measure

Pray for their salvation.

"Brethren, my heart's desire and my prayer to God for them is for their salvation," Paul wrote in Rom. 10:1. Pray—
- that God will bring people into their lives to present the gospel to them
- that Satan will be kept from blinding them to God's wisdom
- for the Holy Spirit to reveal spiritual truth
- for Christian friends for them
- for the church they attend and the people who work with youth their age
- that they will develop a hunger to read God's Word
- that God will draw them to himself

Pray for their future mates.

No matter what the age, pray about whom they will someday marry—
- that they and their future mates are developing a biblical
  view of the role of man and woman, husband and wife
- that they will find mates who have a growing relationship with Jesus Christ
- that their future mates will help them achieve God's
  purpose
- that they will develop a healthy and biblical view of sex
- that they will have the discipline and moral courage to
  control their passions and appetites
- that their mates will come alongside to provide a stable,
  loving, Christian home for your future great-grandchildren

Pray for their careers.
While they are still growing up, pray—
- that they will seek God's wisdom about a future vocation
- that they will find positions that utilize all of their God-
  given gifts and talents
- that they find callings that provide them many spiritual
  opportunities
- that their lives will be given to full-time Christian service
- that those blessed with riches find satisfaction in using
  that wealth for the expansion of God's kingdom

For those who are presently working, pray—
- that they will find God's purpose in their everyday labors
- that they will have the courage to change vocations if
  they sense God's leading in another direction
- that they will build reputations for hard work, loyalty,
  and honesty
- that they will witness to their coworkers of God's grace
  and power

Pray for their wisdom.
Paul had this prayer for the people in Ephesus:

[I pray] that the God of our Lord Jesus Christ, the Father of glory, may give to you a spirit of wisdom and of rev-

elation in the knowledge of Him. I pray that the eyes of your heart may be enlightened, so that you may know what is the hope of His calling, what are the riches of the glory of His inheritance in the saints, and what is the surpassing greatness of His power toward us who believe (*1:17-19*).

What a wonderful prayer to use for our grandchildren!

We don't want our grandkids to merely be the smartest kids in the world—we want them to be the wisest as well. Wisdom is knowing the most godly goal to strive for and the most godly method of achieving that goal. So pray—

- that they will know what to do with their education
- that they will have a balanced view of their beauty, charm, and strength
- that they will know the weaknesses of their own hearts and not trust their own wills
- that they learn to trust the Lord's wisdom above their own

Pray for them in their trials.

Pray—

- that the tough times they face will be turned into sources of spiritual good
- that they will not be embittered by injustices or the power of evil they face
- that they confess their sins
- that they work through to solutions that please God
- that they learn to war against the "rulers, against the powers, against the world forces of this darkness, against the spiritual forces of wickedness in the heavenly places" (Eph. 6:12)
- that they will have just enough trials to keep their trust completely in God's power and grace

Pray for their health and safety.

We all want our grandchildren never to get sick, never to get hurt, never to face any physical pain and struggle. There's nothing wrong in praying for each of these things.

"Beloved, I pray that in all respects you may prosper and be in good health, just as your soul prospers" (3 John 2).

Just keep praying

- for God to heal your grandchildren
- for their parents to be able to make the right treatment decisions
- for the doctors to have the medical knowledge to deal with their situation
- for God to get glory and honor and praise in spite of a health problem
- for your grandchildren to develop lifestyles that are healthy and that will prevent them from suffering many infirmities
- for their safety—at home and in the neighborhood and at school and on the job
- for them to sense God's presence during the scary times
- for them to have the strength of spirit to overcome the fear that Satan will try to bring into their lives

Let them know that you're praying for them.

Never underestimate the power of Grandma and Grandpa's prayers. Just the knowledge that you're praying will act as a loving reminder.

We sat in the bleachers waiting for a football game to begin. A row of college girls sat behind us, and we couldn't help listening in.

"Trish—you're home! How was Italy?"

"It was totally, totally, mega-awesome."

"Oh, yeah? How about the boys?"

"That's what I was talking about."

"Oh! Did you have a lot of dates and stuff?"

"Plenty of dates—but no 'stuff.'"

"Oh, yeah? Are the guys kind of weird?"

"No, they were great."

"But, you didn't even—"

"I didn't even kiss any."

"Really? Why not?"

"I was only there two weeks. Besides, my grandma kept putting the pressure on me."

"You went to Italy with your grandma?"

"Nah, she stayed in her apartment in Los Angeles."

"Well, how did she—?"

"See, on the day I left for Europe she sent me this little card with some money for the trip and a note that said, 'Trish, I know you'll have a great time. I'll be praying for you every day.'"

"Yeah, so what?"

"Well, when my granny says she'll be praying, she means it. She's the type who gets down on her knees and really prays. So I'm over in Italy, and every time I get this notion to go off the wild end, I picture her praying."

"You've go to be kidding!"

"Nope."

"So that ruined your trip?"

"Not really. I had a great time, and I have no regrets. What more could I ask for?"

"I could think of a couple things."

"Yeah, well—I bet you don't have a granny like mine."

Let them see your prayer journal and calendar. Even if they don't have anything to add at the moment, they'll have a visual reminder that you're serious about the business of prayer.

If you have a regular prayer time each week or month for them, let them know when and what time you're in prayer, and what you pray.

"Patrick, I prayed for you last Friday during that tough math test at school. I asked the Lord to allow you to recall all the facts about the math that you've learned and that the test would be an accurate reflection of your true knowledge in the subject."

Throughout the year remind them of your consistent prayers. And when they report to you some result that's an answer to one of your prayers, make sure you give the Lord both private and public gratitude for His graciousness.

Find out what kinds of things they would like you to be praying about.

Your ability to secure this information will certainly vary from grandchild to grandchild. Some will have a handful of requests, often dealing with material possessions that they simply can't live without. Others will rarely have any suggestions.

If they're at your house or around you when you have your prayer journal open, show them their page and then ask, "Is there something you want me to add?"

If they're not around, write a note at least once a year that mentions that you're updating your prayer journal and wonder if they had any special requests.

Keep checking with them year after year even if they never respond to your questions. You want to let them know that your prayers for them will be a consistent, lifetime project. The day may come when they ask for your prayer support. In the meantime, you've established a pattern of true prayer concern.

Share with them your own personal prayer requests.

Whether or not they pray for you will be their decision. But when you ask for their prayers on your behalf, you imply several important lessons. They learn things, such as

Grandparents need prayers too.

You don't have all the answers.

Your Christian life is still growing.

Kids' prayers are important.

We all need each other.

Tell them you're worried about the pain in your left arm and that you would appreciate their prayers next Tuesday when you go to the doctor.

Most kids would appreciate help in knowing how to pray. So you might say in the above case, "Valerie, please pray that the doctors will be able to diagnose the problem quickly and find a treatment that will allow me to continue teaching my Sunday School class." Now they know what to ask the Lord.

Biblical Encouragements to Pray

The Bible is full of exhortations to pray and helps for the praying grandparent:

- Don't lose heart in praying (Luke 18:1-8).
- Pray that your grandchildren won't give in to the many daily temptations (Luke 22:40).

- Even when you aren't sure how to pray for your grandchildren, know that the Holy Spirit will assist you (Rom. 8:26).
- Pray that your grandchildren do no wrong (2 Cor. 13:7).
- Pray that your grandchildren might be made complete, the perfect result of how God intended them to be (2 Cor. 13:9).
- Pray that your grandchildren's love may grow more and more (Phil. 1:9-10).
- Pray that God might count your grandchildren worthy of their calling, in order that the name of the Lord Jesus may be glorified in them (2 Thess. 1:11-12).
- Pray that their faith may not fail (Luke 22:32).
- Pray that they will have strength to escape all the things that are about to take place (Luke 21:36).
- Always thank God for your grandchildren with real joy in your heart for each memory of them He has allowed you to have (Phil. 1:3-4).

The saints of the Bible took prayer seriously. They did not consider it a luxury for the wealthy or the retired. It was to them a solemn duty. To fail to pray was as serious as purposely breaking one of God's commandments.

When Samuel, the aged prophet, priest, and leader of the Hebrew people, decided to retire and allow the new king, Saul, to rule, the people came to him and begged him to keep praying for them.

They were afraid that once he was no longer responsible for the day-to-day leadership of the land, he would withdraw his prayer support as well.

Samuel's answer is classic: "Moreover, as for me, far be it from me that I should sin against the Lord by ceasing to pray for you; but I will instruct you in the good and right way" (1 Sam. 12:23).

Even when they were no longer under his care, even though they now had another leader, even though they might not have a great desire to follow his teaching, Samuel would not even think of abandoning his prayer for them. It was his solemn duty before God.

We can't control our grandkids.

They don't always listen to our counsel and advice.

They may seldom, if ever, write or call or visit, but they still belong to us.

Far be it that we should cease praying for them.

Prayer should be our grandparental passion.

14

The Power of Being a Grandparent Your Grandchildren Can Depend On

Grandparents help kids understand and settle into a world which can be pretty confusing to newcomers.
—Charles Slaybaugh

We sat in the audience at the small elementary school auditorium and waited for the speaker of the evening. It was a rare treat to have a man of such stature visit our rural community. The string of prestigious doctorates that trailed his name in the program shamed the rest of us mortals. He had been president of an eastern university, served two terms as a congressman, and spent time on a presidential commission.

Toward the back, several reporters from nearby newspapers took practice flashes. After a welcome by the school principal and the Pledge of Allegiance, led by a soft-spoken eighth-grade boy, it was time for the introduction of the speaker.

A nine-year-old girl approached the podium. She yanked at the microphone, crackling it down to her level. Then she cleared her throat, which amplified across the room. She giggled and let out a big sigh. The crowd chuckled and also began to relax.

She pulled out a small piece of white paper and carefully unfolded it. With all the dignity possible to a nine-year-old, she took a deep breath and began.

"Fellow students, teachers and staff, parents, ladies and gentlemen, it gives me great pleasure to introduce to you . . ."

There was a slight pause. The perky young lady broke into a wide grin.

"My grandpa!"

She grabbed up the paper, spun around on the platform, gave a big hug to the honored guest, and sat down.

The crowd broke into a thunderous ovation. We weren't clapping for the eminent scholar, statesman, and celebrity. We were clapping for this little girl's grandfather.

When the crowd settled down and the man regained his composure, he wiped back a tear and quietly said, "I've never had a better introduction than that."

We're sure he's right. Is there any higher acclaim than to see the shine in the eyes and face of a youngster who yells with utter abandonment, "Hi, Grandma! Hi, Grandpa!"

One of the warmest benedictions in Scripture is found in Ps. 128:6—"Indeed, may you see your children's children." It was a powerful motivation in the lives of the ancient Hebrews, and it remains powerful today.

Not only should grandparents be able to get to know their grandchildren, but the reverse is true as well. We must be the kind of grandparents our grandkids can count on. We must strive for a level of stability that builds confidence and trust in the next generation and the generations to come.

Many of us are convinced that we need to play an important part in our grandchildren's lives, but we're not sure where to begin. One good thing about being a grandparent is that you can't be fired. You can just muddle along with no direction or purpose, hoping everything turns out fine. You'll still be called Grandpa, and you'll probably still receive another tie for Christmas.

But for you that may not be good enough. You're determined to do more.

However, a book like this can present so many ideas that you feel overwhelmed. Here's what we suggest.

Shore Up Your Spiritual Life

No matter where you are in your walk with the Lord, give it a thorough examination. Hold your life up to the mirror of Scripture and see if you like the reflection.

Paul said a person should not "think more highly of himself than he ought to think; but to think so as to have sound judgment" (Rom. 12:3).

Meditate on your failures, and face up to them. Depend on a second-chance God to bring good out of any mess you hand Him. Rebuild some good Bible study habits, rekindle an active prayer practice, get back into a Bible study group. Try an old-fashioned spring cleaning of your spiritual priorities.

Mend Some Fences

Are there broken relationships in your family? Maybe they're just strained. Reach out where God directs to reseal bonds if at all possible. A good grandparent must at least try.

Jesus stated a similar principle when He said, "If you are presenting your offering at the altar, and there remember that your brother has something against you, leave your offering there before the altar and go; first be reconciled to your brother, and then come and present your offering" (Matt. 5:23-24).

If the strife or animosity is deep, longstanding, and far spread, seek divine direction to know where to start. Determine what healing is needed most for the grandchildren's sake.

Pick Out One of the Communication Projects

If you keep saying things like "I haven't talked to the grandkids in a long time" or "I know I ought to write to them more often," start there.

Right now you could lay down this book and go write that letter or E-mail or make that phone call.

Not tomorrow. Not this week. Not soon. Now.

Look for a Weak Relationship

A good place to begin is the relationship that needs the most help. Maybe you have a grandson in the service and haven't seen him in years. Maybe there's a granddaughter in Alaska whom you've never seen. Has some barrier come between you and your grandchildren?

Abraham's grandson Jacob tried to live up to his name, "the deceiver" or "the trickster." He bartered with his brother, Esau, plotted with his mother, Rebekah, lied to his father, Isaac, and finally had to flee the Promised Land. But he returned years later and raised his large family. When his favorite son, Joseph, was sold off by his brothers, Jacob mourned for years after being told he was dead.

But his life didn't end with that sorrow. There was a day when he was finally reunited with Joseph, a day when they fell on each other's necks and wept (Gen. 46:29). And there is no more touching scene:

> When Israel [Jacob] saw Joseph's sons, he said, "Who are these?" Joseph said to his father, "They are my sons, whom God has given me here." So he said, "Bring them to me, please, that I may bless them." Now the eyes of Israel were so dim from age that he could not see. Then Joseph brought them close to him, and he kissed them and embraced them. Israel said to Joseph, "I never expected to see your face, and behold, God has let me see your children as well" *(48:8-11)*.

Maybe you have some grandchildren you think you'll never see again. Hang in there. Don't give up. Start working from your side of things to reestablish those relationships.

Tackle One Project at a Time

"It's too much! I can't do all this," you might complain. Like anything else, we do our grandparenting one step at a time. And we don't have to allow past mistakes to prevent us from trying something new.

We've probably done a lot of things right. That doesn't mean we can't nudge ourselves to try a little harder.

Flip back through each chapter of this book to review various topics, and hone in on certain sections you feel you can incorporate into your life. You may want to try one idea that attracts you more than the others. That's where to begin.

Relax about everything else and go with that one project. The others will wait until next week, next month, or next year.

Jesus once said, "You are to be perfect, as your heavenly Father is perfect" (Matt. 5:48).

In a spiritual sense, we are made perfect (complete), in God's eyes, when we accept Christ and are given His righteousness. But down here on earth regarding God's ideal for us, we're not made instantly perfect. We grow in the process of such perfection. We conform one area of life to His standard. Then add another and then another, until we reach "the measure of the stature which belongs to the fullness of Christ" (Eph. 4:13).

Have Fun

We just came back from our county fair. When you live in a county of 4,000 people, the fair is a small event but a big deal. We watched with delight as county youngsters showed their home-raised animals.

The winner of the intermediate class of showing and fitting sheep was an 11-year-old friend of ours. She was thrilled to win the big ribbon, and we celebrated with her. As the judge explained why he selected that particular girl, he concluded with these words: "The only thing I would have liked to have seen different was the girl's expression. It would have been great to see a smile. I like to think the kids are having fun."

Hannah was so intensely engrossed in the competition that she forgot to smile.

Grandmas and grandpas can be that way too. We can get so intense with accomplishing what we think are God's goals that we make the whole process a chore. Relationships aren't meant to be that way.

Go back to Prov. 17:6—"Grandchildren are the crown of old men." The crown. The royalty. The splendor. The very object you want to show off to others.

Married young, she never finished high school. Society would call her unskilled by today's standards. Besides raising a family, she cooked meals for 50 hungry ranch hands. She made her own soap, cranked a wringer washer, and rolled a piecrust that would melt in your mouth.

Soft spoken, mild mannered, agreeable almost to a fault, we used to think of her as a little naive. But then we realized that at some point in her many years, she deliberately chose to see life that way. She not only hoped and prayed that everything would turn out well—she counted on it.

There was nothing she wouldn't bake for her grandkids. There was nothing in her modest home she wouldn't give to any who even hinted they had need for it. And as far as she was concerned, there was nothing her grandchildren couldn't accomplish. She just knew she had three brilliant grandchildren.

When Granny died, she didn't leave a vast estate. There wasn't much left that she hadn't already given away. What was left was a little one-bedroom house on the poorer side of town, a 30-year-old sofa, and some fancy embroidered pillowcases. Not much else.

She did leave her three grandchildren with a lifetime of loving, laughing memories.

Two are now ministers of the gospel, helping others find the Lord. The third is a gifted schoolteacher and administrator, encouraging little ones to learn.

Granny would be proud—plumb proud.

We can survive without grandparents, but it's a much poorer life indeed.

Remember Prov. 13:22? "A good man leaves an inheritance to his children's children."

Being the kind of grandparent your grandkids can count on—that's a legacy every grandparent on earth has an equal chance to leave.